C

M000084236

The simplified code name of NELL worked far better for the Allies than having to call this airplane a Mitsubishi Navy Type 96 Land Based Attacker.

JAPANESE AIRCRAFT

Code Names & Designations

Robert C. Mikesh

Schiffer Military/Aviation History
Atglen, PA

Frank T. McCoy Jr.
Major General, USAF (Ret.)

Foreword

As we talked that morning in early 1942, we could not have realized the impact that our new idea would make by assigning simple to remember nicknames to Japanese aircraft. Our work in air intelligence when first assigned in Australia soon after the Pacific War began, was to gather intelligence information about the Japanese aircraft. We had little or nothing with which to start. Each airplane discovered seemed to have a strange sounding name to us, none of which had any meaning. One thing that was fairly consistent in reported sightings of Japanese aircraft by Allied aircrews was that if they were fighters, they were called "Zeros."

Fran (Francis) Williams, a first-rate top-drawer intelligence specialist, was my NCO working with me on Air Intelligence at the time and we discussed the idea of using "nicknames" by which to identify Japanese airplanes. How it evolved so simply to use easy to remember first names of people we do not recall, but the male/female name system obviously worked well since it prevails even today.

It was important that our aircrews report accurately what they were up against. To know the difference between a **Zeke** or an **Oscar** meant that the combat crews when meeting a **Zeke** knew that they were facing the best pilots and equipment that Japan had to offer. Identifying the fighter as an **Oscar** meant that it was less vulnerable than **Zeke** because of its armor plate and self sealing tanks. Usually it had a less competent pilot. Identifying these airplanes with a simple to use name, conveyed a lot of information to the well informed.

Our intent was to select names for brevity and of such a sequence of letters that would not be easily garbled in tele-communications or voice transmissions. As the code names, or nicknames, became more widely used, suggestions and use of new code names made by the Navy, Australians, British and Free Allied Forces were coordinated with London, Washington and the CBI before they were assigned. Admittedly, some personal preferences with regards to some of our friends and relatives were bound to creep into the system, but there were relatively few.

The use of code names did not end here with the Japanese aircraft of the Pacific War. While we were engaged in the Cold War with the Soviet Union, the NATO forces had the same problem with strange sounding and difficult to spell names of Soviet aircraft. As a result, I was placed on temporary duty at the Air Defense Command Headquarters in Colorado Springs shortly after it was established. My purpose was to discuss the feasibility of code names for Russian aircraft with Brigadier General W.M. "Woody" Burgess, their A-2 (assistant chief of staff for intelligence). Burgess had been Deputy Director for Intelligence at Headquarters USAF, and I had worked under him in 1944 when we organized all Technical Air Intelligence. The result of our discussions brought about the NATO code names for Russian aircraft, another simple method that was soon implemented.

The simplest systems are the ones that last. It is my hope that this book that covers so thoroughly this subject of Japanese aircraft code names and how this all began will serve as a reference source for any future need for this type of identification system.

Frank T. McCoy, Jr.
Major General, USAF (Ret.)

Book Design by Robert Biondi

First Edition
Copyright © 1993 by Robert C. Mikesh.
Library of Congress Catalog Number: 92-85346

All rights reserved. No part of this work may be reproduced or used in any forms or by
any means – graphic, electronic or mechanical, including photocopying or information
storage and retrieval systems – without written permission from the copyright holder.

Printed in the United States of America.
ISBN: 0-88740-447-2

We are interested in hearing from authors with book ideas on related topics.

Published by Schiffer Publishing Ltd.
77 Lower Valley Road
Atglen, PA 19310
Please write for a free catalog.
This book may be purchased from the publisher.
Please include $2.95 postage.
Try your bookstore first.

Contents

Preface

The use of Japanese aircraft code names in lieu of their Official and Project Designations has been a preferred method of describing these airplanes since this system was developed in July 1942. Over the years that have followed, a listing of these code names (or nicknames) and their corresponding Japanese identities has been published in relatively accurate and complete form. No one air intelligence listing contained all these names because over the wartime period, some names were dropped and new ones added. With this passing of time, however, this early source material becomes less available, and the few people that once knew these details are long removed from these matters. New material lost within files has also come to light, adding more insight to the overall story about these names.

It is for this and other reasons that a new consolidation of this material has been put together by this author. In addition, a subject seldom touched upon has to do with recording who some of the name sakes were from which these nicknames evolved. With the assistance of the two people that were the prime assigners of these names, twenty-six of these names have association with real people, many of which are described here for the first time. These personal associations were certainly not to be part of the code name assignments, but some connections were bound to happen.

In the early years following World War II, the code names continued to be used, but it was not until 1966 that a meaningful coverage of the subject was put together in the book *Japanese Code Names,* World War I Aero Publishers, Inc., authored by Richard M. Bueschel. It was Bueschel that first broke the ice by making known to the English language readers the first meaningful glimpses into the background of Japanese aviation material, an interest now shared by many. That first list also appears as an appendix in *Japanese Aircraft of the Pacific War,* by Rene J. Francillon, as well as several reprints of Bueschel's material in aviation magazines.

It is with the compiling of this book, that additional intelligence documents have come to be known, expanding this listing with even new names such as **Clint, John, Maisie** and **Joan**. The discovery of errors in some name assignments reversed with others could have been printer errors. These have resulted in major changes in descriptions that primarily affect **Abdul, Doris, Harry,** and **Norma**.

In addition to this new coverage of Japanese aircraft code names, this book contains as a cross reference to these names, their associated Official and Project Designations. So often a researcher will remember an airplane being a "Type 99," or a "Model J1N something," or just as "**Sam**," and needs a more positive form of identification. This book has been designed so that it will serve this much needed cross reference source for this information. Great care has been taken in recording as precisely as possible the correct wordage in these nomenclatures used within these very complicated Japanese systems.

An effort like this cannot be that of one person. With regards to the code name system and its background, this coverage could not be complete without the untiring cooperation of the two men that actually developed the system and made the initial name assignments. The officer in charge was Frank T. McCoy, Jr. of Nashville, Tennessee, a Captain then, and retired in 1968 as Major General, USAF (Ret). During his Air Force career, he occupied positions as Chief, Technical Division, ACAS/Intelligence, later as Deputy Asst. Secretary of the Air

Force and thereafter at Headquarters Tactical Air Command. McCoy was aided by the "idea man" Francis "Fran" Williams who now resides in Rio Rancho, New Mexico. He made the system work. Williams remained in air Intelligence work throughout the war as well as the Korean War, retiring as a Technical Air Intelligence Warrant Officer in 1973. He was the first, and for several years, the only warrant in the Air Force with that specialty. Over the past several years these two men willingly gave of their time and knowledge to put this work together in the most complete form possible. Both of these officers lost track of Joe Grattan of their initial team of three, sometime after the team was dispersed. As Williams said in one of his most recent letters following endless reviews of this material for completeness and accuracy, "perhaps we can now dot the last "i" and put this subject to bed once and for all!"

Already mentioned is Richard M. Bueschel, who is really the pioneer of the subject of Japanese aircraft of World War II. In addition to numerous air intelligence documents that were reviewed for this new coverage, it was Bueschel's original publication upon which this new book was based.

My sincere thanks not only go to the above named gentlemen, but to others as well that reviewed selected details for which they were of great help. Shorzoe Abe is always my mentor in Japanese aviation subjects, and has reviewed this work from the Japanese perspective. Dr. James H. Kitchens, III reviewed certain Air Force Documents at the Office of Air Force History that helped confirm critical details. James F. Lansdale, James I. Long and Frank J. Olynyk provided invaluable assistance by reviews, comments and additional information that was greatly appreciated. My dear wife, Ramona, continues to tolerate these endless hours of work, and lends a very helpful hand at seeing that this material is in a presentable form. To all of these people, and others that have been a part of this tedious project, I extend my sincerest thanks.

Robert C. Mikesh
Washington, D.C.
1992

Chapter I
What's In a Name?

In any discussion about Japanese aircraft of World War II, names such as **Zeke**, **Betty**, **Oscar**, **Kate** and more are generally used to describe these airplanes. Even the Japanese in modern day conversations often refer to their airplanes with these Allied assigned code names, instead of as an example: Aichi Navy Type 99 Carrier Bomber Model 11. The code name **Val**, describes the same airplane (or to be more specific **Val 11**). This system of American names for these Japanese airplanes is well accepted, but few users realize that many of these names relate to real people. While this was not the intent for this system, some personality link-ups would naturally take place – quite unofficially – yet it was considered an honor to feel that one's name had been specifically selected for one of these airplanes. Few backgrounds of these names have ever been recorded, but with the assistance of those that bestowed these names, here for the first time is the most complete story of who some of these people were.

The newest of the Japanese bombers in the opening months of the war was the Mitsubishi G4M1 that the Allies code named BETTY. It was distinguishable by its cigar shaped fuselage, single tail and pronounced gun blisters.

One of the better known Japanese bombers was given the name of **Betty**. Although the name selections were being made in Australia, the real Betty was an attractive American nurse from Bridgeville, Pennsylvania, described as being *well endowed*. How better to have a name that relates well to this bomber, with its large blister gun positions than to name this one **Betty**!

This easy to remember system of naming Japanese aircraft had a very logical purpose. At the beginning of the war in the Southwest Pacific, generally all Japanese fighters were identified as a "Zero" or if they were bombers they had a choice of calling them "Mitsubishis" or "Nakajimas." The more flamboyant aircrews after a major air engagement may have worked into the report having seen "Kawanishis" as well. There was no formula for differentiating among types because there was no method of designating them. The result was confusion in any reference being made to Japanese aircraft. One thing for sure, if it had what was often described as a "red meatball" insignia, it was Japanese.

Up to the time America entered the war, only a shadow of a formal technical intelligence system existed for the collection of information concerning potential enemies. What gathering capability did exist rested in the hands of a few attaches spread throughout the world. But once gathered, there was little mechanism for putting the information in the hands of those that needed it. There was no central agency that was an authority on aircraft of potential enemies. Consequently, when Japanese aircraft were met in combat and reported, there was no system by which to identify them in order to evaluate their capabilities. As example, initially there was a standing order "do not dogfight with a **Zeke** fighter" but the type had to be identified first to those involved.

The problem for clearing up this dilemma was taken on by the Materiel Section of the Directorate of Intelligence, Allied Air Forces, Southwest Pacific Area, located in Victoria Barracks, Melbourne, Australia in the early days of the Pacific War. One of the key figures charged with this task to create order out of this chaos, and in disseminating this information about Japanese aircraft, was Frank T. McCoy Jr., of Nashville, Tennessee. As a Captain, he went to Australia early in 1942 with the 38th Bombardment Group, as their intelligence officer. The overall problem of gathering intelligence information was greater than at group level, so he was further assigned to fill the new position as "Materiel Officer" in the Allied

Colonel Frank T. McCoy Jr, left, discusses the newly rebuilt HAMP fighter with his engineering officer Major Clyde Gessel as the airplane was being prepared for its first test flight at Eagle Farm Airfield, Brisbane. McCoy and his staff in Australia had primary responsibility for assigning the Japanese aircraft code names.

Air Force, Southwest Pacific Area Headquarters intelligence organization at Melbourne. With him, having come from their stateside assignment at Jackson Army Air Base, Mississippi, was his senior intelligence specialist, Technical Sergeant Francis M. "Fran" Williams. A third person making up this team and one who also had a part in this coding system of Japanese airplanes was Corporal Joseph Grattan. He primarily handled the many clerical duties associated with this task for the unit.

According to Fran Williams, the idea of code names surfaced one morning when he and McCoy were discussing the tangled mess of trying to identify Japanese airplanes. Even if Japan's official list of aircraft designations were at hand, they would be of little help, for the Japanese Army and Navy used separate systems, both having their own long complicated jargon as well as a short form, and neither having a resemblance to the other. These designations were seldom learned until well after the new type was encountered in combat. Initially, the Americans began with a Serial Number assignment recognition/identification system, but with little meaningful success.

There was nothing glamorous or startling over the new idea that sparked assigning simple, easy to remember names of people to these airplanes. By our very nature, Americans must put things into categories, so they decided that fighters and float planes would be given "boy's" names, as they called them, and bombers, reconnaissance aircraft, and flying boats, and anything else left over, would have "girl's" names. Later it would be further refined so that names used for transports would begin with "T" and trainers would have tree names. Still later, gliders were given names of birds. That seemed simple enough at the moment, so the pairing of names with aircraft for which something was known about them began in July 1942.

McCoy's home state was Tennessee, so the first of the names in the series emerged with distinctly hillbilly nicknames such as **Zeke**, **Rufe**, **Jake**, **Nate**, and **Pete**; short, simple and easy to remember, and not prone to be garbled in tele-communications. Tying the name **Zeke** to the Zero Fighter was a natural pairing. The short list of hillbilly names was soon exhausted. Selecting additional names then became more methodical and the natural element emerged in that the team thought about people they knew, and began putting real people and their names with these airplanes.

Frank McCoy did just that on the right occasions. To recognize his wife in the code name series, **Louise** got tagged to an airplane they carried on the books as the Army Mitsubishi Ki-2 Type 93 Light Bomber. Little were they to know that this antiquated airplane had been out of service for several years, but it kept appearing in popular aviation magazines. This was no reflection directed to his wife, McCoy is quick to point out. The lack of information that Allied intelligence had to go with at the beginning of the war was unbelievable. There was little else to draw upon but old Japanese magazines. Jane's All the World Aircraft carried only sketchy information, but it added something from which to start gathering more detailed information.

Because of this, the more obvious aircraft known to the Allies were the most obsolete because of Japanese censorship over their newer types. As a result, their careful naming of aircraft after their friends and relatives, became the majority of names that were seldom, if ever used. Some of these airplanes were fictitious from the start, yet not learned until much later. One such airplane was the so called Mitsubishi T.K.4 Type O Special Fighter, one with which Frank McCoy tagged with his own first name. From the modern lines of this airplane shown in a published sketch, this would surely be met in combat and one to be dealt with. How then were these Americans to know that the sketch they saw that somewhat resembled a Fokker D.XXIII, was really a "dream design" in this Japanese model airplane magazine? Other designs from available news sources, not known at the time to be fictitious, were given the names of **Gus**, **Omar**, and regrettably; **Joe**, for team member Joe Grattan, whose name therefore remained in the records, but obviously not in connection with an actual airplane due to this hasty allocation that became a mistake.

Frank McCoy recovered the use of his name from a fictitious aircraft later in the war, however. This name of **Frank** was ultimately assigned to an Army fighter that became very active and widely known, the Nakajima Ki-84 Hayate. The name **Harry**, borrowed from Colonel Harry Cunningham, a friend of McCoy's that worked for General Ennis Whitehead as his A-2 at Advon 5AF at Port Moresby, New Guinea, was substituted for the earlier usage of **Frank** for which Cunningham's name was assigned. As for his friend Whitehead, McCoy recalls, "the name Ennis just didn't seem to fit with an airplane."

June was a code name that was also prematurely used. This happened to be McCoy's only daughter at that time. The dive bomber **Val** was already a recognized type, and when a twin-float airplane of nearly the same lines was spotted, it was thought to be a **Val** on floats. Thinking this too was a bomber, it rightfully should have a girl's name. He used daughter June's name for this airplane, and the information about this new enemy aircraft was circulated throughout the war zone. After the capture of one, and discovering it to be an entirely different type that had already rightfully been given a boys name for float planes; **Paul**, the name **June** had to be shelved.

Tending to keep things in the family, McCoy's mother in law's name Clara was thought to be assigned to a sure thing. In a captured Japanese document was a picture of what was to be the replacement for the Ki-46 **Dinah**; the Tachikawa Ki-70 Command Reconnaissance-plane. The airplane became a disappointment in early development, and only three prototypes

were ever built, yet the code name **Clara** remained assigned.

Fran Williams fell into this early rush of name assignments which included the naming of the **Betty** bomber as previously described. He attached his own name **Francis** to an airplane found in reports of sighting a new twin-engine heavy fighter. This airplane was nimble and fast as reported, but it turned out to be a bomber, the Kugisho (Yokosuka) P1Y1 Navy Bomber Ginga. Recognizing now that it rightfully required a feminine name, only the spelling of this name had to be changed to **Frances**, making it correct, but this left Williams also without an airplane namesake.

A key staffer in the Japanese code name system was M/Sgt Francis "Fran" Williams. Once the plan was set in motion, it was Williams that propelled the system and made it work, making many of the name selections and assigning them to specific aircraft.

What's in a Name?   13

Williams assigned his name FRANCIS to this Kugisho P1Y1 when it was first reported as being a fighter. Later when discovered to be a bomber, the masculine name spelling had to be changed to the feminine gender for bombers to become FRANCES.

While off duty in Brisbane, Australia, Joe Grattan writes a letter to his fiancee, Ida, both first names of which were used for Japanese aircraft code names. Grattan was one of the original three air intelligence team members that developed the Japanese airplane code names.

The unit's administrative technician, Joe Grattan had left a girlfriend behind with plans of marrying when he got back from the war. Her name, **Ida**, was soon attached to the Tachikawa Ki-36, Direct Co-operation Plane, an aircraft with a fixed landing gear, later used as an advanced trainer as the Ki-55. As a matter of interest, Joe and Ida did get married when the war was over.

Down the hall from where this team worked in the intelligence section was an attractive WAAF by the name of Joyce Gillie. How better to attract her attention than for Fran Williams to make conversation by asking if she would mind if he used her name of **Joyce** to identify a Japanese plane? With a trace of a blush and a perky smile, she consented. This was assigned to what was thought to be an Army Type 1 Light Bomber of mistaken identity with a type already named; the Mitsubishi Ohtori **Eve**.

Little can be seen here of Joyce Gillie at the piano in Australia, an attractive WAAF assigned to the air intelligence unit. Her name JOYCE was applied to what was thought to be an Army Type 1 Light Bomber found later to have been previously named EVE.

There were few exceptions where code names once assigned to an airplane were changed. When that did happen, there were what some thought to be good reason. One example is the name **Hamp** that was applied to the clipped wing version of the Zero, the A6M3 Model 32. When this was first spotted, it was presumed to be a new fighter type of the Japanese. In honor of General H.H. "Hap" Arnold, USAAF commanding general, his nickname was used. Back in Washington, as the story was told, when an intelligence briefing was being given to the General, the report was made that a large number of **Haps** were being shot down or destroyed on the ground in the New Guinea area. With this mention of his name, Arnold is reported to have asked sharply, "Where did it get that name **Hap**?" The young briefing officer, detecting what he thought was displeasure, quickly replied that "we are in the process of getting that changed, General!" Nothing further was said to learn if Arnold was pleased or disappointed with the name change, but messages were sent to Australia to the effect that the change must be made. To do so, and to avoid as much confusion in name swapping as possible, the name was modified to **Hamp**, "in honor of one of the air heroes in the China theater," according to a dispatch. This change was announced in the December 1943 Recognition Journal. Eventually that name was even dropped in favor of **Zeke 32**, since it was in fact another model of the Zero Fighter.

This raises the question as to who this ace with the name "Hamp" might be after which this aircraft was named? In a message dated 12 April 1944, from Headquarters Allied Air

When this airplane, the Mitsubishi Navy Type 0 Carrier Based Fighter Model 32 was first encountered, it was thought to be a new type because of its squared wing tips. First named HAP, it was later changed to HAMP, in honor of downed CBI ace John Hampshire.

Captain John F. Hampshire, Jr had just achieved his thirteenth air victory over China on May 2, 1943 when he was forced to land his P-40 in a river and soon died of wounds. His peers, having learned of the name problem with HAP that was to be changed, asked that an "m" be added in honor of their fallen friend "Hamp" Hampshire.

Forces (USAF HRC 703.168, Mar-Apr 1944. Fifth AF. Corresp. File. USAF History Office) describing the code naming program, it touched on the earlier renaming of Hap. In that description it states; "However, China suggested one of their aces, whose first name was HAMP, be tagged with a code name; and the "m" was inserted." The number of U.S. fighter aces in the CBI by mid-1943 was not all that large and made such a search quite conclusive. The list (USAF Credits for the Destruction of Enemy Aircraft, WW II, USAF Historical Study No.85, 1978) showed that Captain John F. Hampshire, Jr. of Grant's Pass, Oregon, bagged his thirteenth victory on May 2, 1943. While returning to his home base, deteriorating weather and the shortage of fuel caused "Hamp" (as he was called by his friends), to ditch his P-40 in a river near Changsha. Although rescued, he soon died of abdominal injuries. As the CBI's leading ace at that time, Hampshire had to have been the "leading ace" referred to, therefore the renaming of this model of the Zero was in his honor.

One of the biplane-types frequently pictured in magazines was the Nakajima B4Y1 Type 96 Carrier Attack Plane. This was the type aircraft expected in any opening attacks of the war instead of the modern torpedo bomber **Kate**. Frank McCoy came up with the code name **Jean**, thinking of Jean Faircloth MacArthur (the wife of General Douglas MacArthur), who had lived near his hometown in Murfreesboro, Tennessee. These airplanes had been active in the Sino-Japanese war but served only as trainers during the Pacific War.

For the Mitsubishi Ki-21 Heavy Bomber, the name **Sally** was selected. Frank McCoy had a close working relationship with his former 38th Bomb Group commander, Fay R. Upthegrove, later a Major General. Upthegrove did not leave the United States with the 38th when they departed on January 31, 1942 for Australia, but instead took command positions in the European Theater and became recognized there as a war hero. McCoy's earlier close association with Upthegrove and his wife, prompted the use of her name **Sally**, for this bomber that is popularly known by that name.

Another friend of McCoy's was Captain Ray W. McDuffey, later retired Colonel, USAF. McDuffey got out of the Philippines in the early days of the war and made it to Melbourne where he became instrumental in developing combat intelligence in the 5th Air Force and later in the Allied Air Forces Headquarters. He came from Portland, Oregon, as a former school teacher, and had a great sense of humor, according to McCoy. Nothing would do but to assign his name **Ray** to a Japanese fighter that was spotted and reported by the CBI (China Burma India) Theater Intelligence personnel. As time passed, it was learned that the airplane spotted was a Zero, already assigned the name **Zeke** and the code name **Ray** had to be dropped.

The officer in charge of the Japanese aircraft code naming system, Frank T. McCoy applied his name to one of the early identified aircraft. As FRANK, this reported twin-engine single-seat fighter soon turned out to be somebodies "dream aircraft" found in a Japanese magazine.

The McDuffey's were not out of the picture yet, however. Ray's wife Nell, has the honor of her name being assigned to the Mitsubishi G3M Navy Type 96 Attack Bomber. This was the Japanese Navy's most versatile bomber in the early part of the war. Before the war, civil airplanes of this type made long distance international good will flights to points in Europe and the United States. As a bomber and in defiance of a typhoon, **Nells** made history with deep penetration attacks into the heartland of China from bases on Kyushu, the southern most home island of Japan. These attack missions made this the first transoceanic bombing operation in the history of aerial warfare. This surprising event of two days running, shocked the world, yet Japan was not taken seriously as having a world class air power for the war she was prepared to undertake.

Other friends of McCoy had their names used as well, but too often prematurely. Many airplane types were generated from hand sketches made by air crews to describe what they saw in combat. To what was described as the Nagoya-Sento KI-001 fighter was given the name **Ben**. This was Frank McCoy's "boss" at that time, Major Benjamin B. Cain, later Colonel as the FEAF A-2 (Far East Air Force, intelligence chief). As it turned out, this airplane was also a misidentified Zero and this name too had to be dropped.

One of the code names of Japanese aircraft that prominently sticks in the minds of code name users is that of **Val**. This name was assigned to the fixed landing gear Aichi D3A1 dive

When this Nakajima Army Ki-84 Hayate came on the scene late in the war, Frank McCoy withdrew his name from the inactive list of aircraft and assigned FRANK to this impressive fighter. The FRANK aircraft was regarded as the Japanese best Army fighter in operational service.

bomber that played so prominently in the attack on Pearl Harbor. McCoy came up with this one which related to an Australian while this naming was taking place in Melbourne. Val was an Australian Army sergeant that became a close friend of Major Ben Cain, McCoy's boss.

An airplane similar to **Val**, also having a pronounced fixed and well-faired landing gear, was reported early in the war as being seen in Southeast Asia. The intelligence gathering team determined this to be the Mitsubishi Type 97-2 Carrier Attack Bomber, and added yet another airplane to the ever increasing list of enemy aircraft types. As another bomber, it needed a feminine name. McCoy had already expended family names, so now his mind searched for friend's names from his past. Close college friends are seldom forgotten, and Mabel from the University of Oklahoma where they both attended came to mind. The name of **Mabel** was used, but like so many airplanes at this early time period, this one was soon relegated to ancillary duties and was not among the popular types.

Written and visual information about Japanese aircraft was in limited supply to this intelligence team in Australia. Having access to some 1938 Japanese magazines they noted that much attention was being given to a tri-motored twin-float bomber that was frequently pictured. Anticipating this type to become a new Japanese aircraft being contemplated for production, the code name **Ione** was assigned to it. This namesake was that of Ione Belvin, wife of Major Charles H. Belvin who was another close friend of McCoy's. Belvin was an engineer, formerly in the 38th Bomb Group to which they both had been assigned, later assigned to the 5th Air Force Air Service Command (ASC) in Australia. McCoy "borrowed" him from ASC after obtaining an order from the 5th Air Force Chief of Staff directing ASC to release him for temporary duty with McCoy's intelligence unit. Belvin led natives in teams throughout the Pacific islands to recover downed Japanese airplanes for their study by intelligence personnel. McCoy relates that there was no recovery too difficult that Charley Belvin could not accomplish. As for the aircraft **Ione**, it was obviously similar to the Italian Cantieri Riuniti dell' Adriatico (CANT) Z.506B which suggests that it was a misinterpretation made from these magazines, for no Japanese aircraft of this type ever appeared, yet it remained in recognition manuals until early 1943.

Some Australians were brought into the application of code names. A friend of McCoy's in Australia, by the name of **Claude**, whose last name has vanished with time, used his name to identify the Mitsubishi A5M, spatted landing gear low-wing Navy fighter. This astounding airplane was the world's first monoplane carrier based fighter, a trend that other navies did not quickly follow, but proved most successful.

Another Australian that worked closely with this intelligence activity was George Vivian Remmington. As a Flight Sergeant in the Royal Australian Air Force, he was an illustrator for the air intelligence unit and the one initially responsible for making the silhouette drawings of these airplanes to be used in recognition training and differentiating one type from another. His impeccable work was seen by anyone having to do with recognizing Japanese aircraft types and their associated code names. Fortunately, his name was not applied too early in the war. **George** became the nickname for the land version of the single float **Rex** seaplane fighter, that saw considerable action against attacking B-29s.

Squadron Leader Norm Clappison, RAAF, former commissioner at Rabaul, and field team leader with an air intelligence unit team has his name on the code list, but on an airplane with little activity. The airplane carrying his name; **Norm** was what looked to be the promising Kawanishi E15K1 Shiun Reconnaissance Seaplane. This powerful single float two-place airplane with retractable wing tip floats was too complex for its time, including its

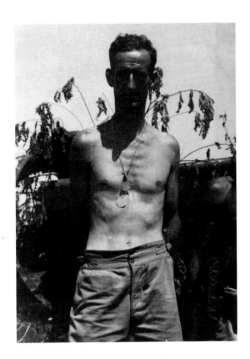

George Remmington was a Flight Sergeant in the RAAF and assigned as part of the air intelligence team. He was an excellent draftsman, making 3-view drawings of the Japanese airplanes from any information available, often taking his own measurements in the field. His name of GEORGE was assigned to the Kawanishi N1K1-J Navy fighter.

Much recognition for success in recovering downed Japanese aircraft for study was because of Squadron Leader Norm Clappison, RAAF. He knew the Southwest Pacific islands well and could recruit, train and organize the New Guinea natives (background) for efforts to recover Japanese aircraft for intelligence use.

When the Kawanishi N1K1-J first appeared as a land based fighter, it was not immediately recognized as an adaptation of the N1K1 Seaplane Fighter. It was deserving of a code name of its own and was assigned GEORGE to recognize the work of team member Flight Sergeant George Remmington, RAAF.

To acknowledge Norm Clappison's contribution to the air intelligence effort, his name was assigned to this Kawanishi E15K High-speed Reconnaissance Seaplane. The airplane as a type failed to be fully developed and become operational, so little use was given to the name NORM.

engine with two counter-rotating propellers. Few remember Norm Clappison by this airplane but Fran Williams remembers him as a fine and courageous officer, a person to whom they were much indebted for his success in the intelligence gathering from downed aircraft. Norm knew the islands of the Southwest Pacific well. He recruited, trained and organized the New Guinea natives who were so vital in the recovery of Japanese aircraft and associated parts.

By mid-1942, the intelligence unit moved from Melbourne to Brisbane, taking up residence at the newly constructed airfield called Eagle Farm. It was here that the recovered

The focal point of Allied air intelligence and the code naming of Japanese aircraft was this Hangar No. 7 at Eagle Farm airport, now part of Brisbane International Airport. As of 1991, this building has been designated a historic land mark because of its use and activities held there during World War II.

Japanese aircraft and equipment was brought for rebuilding and testing. This effort received the strong support of General George C. Kenney, Commander of 5th Air Force and Allied Air Forces Pacific. Kenney had a strong background with engineering experience at Wright-Patterson Field and therefore recognized the need of the information to be gained. It was he that authorized and directed the construction of Hangar 7 at Eagle Farm, a facility that became well known yet highly restricted because of the rebuilding and testing of Japanese airplanes that went on there. (As of 1991, this hangar at what is now Brisbane International Airport has been designated a historical building for retention).

New Japanese aircraft frequently came to the team's attention at this intelligence gathering facility. One of these, the Kokusai Ki-59 Army Type 1 Transport had been identified and needed a code name. Working for the intelligence unit was an Australian secretary that Williams gave some attention to, and **Theresa** became that new code name. She was fortunate that her name began with a "T," because soon after the code name designations system was started, it was decided to further categorize the system by assigning names for transports that start with a "T."

There were exceptions to this, however. For example the code names of **Tojo** and **Tony**. The fighter that was named **Tojo** was first encountered in the CBI and so named by the combatants there. In another theater, believed to be the S.W.P.A., it was seemingly given the nickname of **John**, but a formal request was made to retain the name **Tojo** since it was already so widely known. This was approved.

When the airplane that ultimately was given the name **Tony** was first seen, its in-line engine gave the impression that it could be an Italian design since it closely resembled the Macchi MC 202. It was later realized that this was purely a Japanese design, but before this was learned, the name **Tony**, with its Italian connotation was given to the Kawasaki Ki-61 Hien.

Other thought-to-be foreign designs got names as well. The news media picked up on the point that small numbers of German aircraft of varying types were being exported to Japan. It was not unusual that the Japanese made efforts to purchase the latest designs from other countries to compare and test their own designs against the tops in world technology. Assuming that one would be Germany's latest fighter, the Focke-Wulf Fw 190, the similar sounding name of **Fred** was assigned. It was not until the summer of 1943 that a single Fw 190A5 reached Japan, yet it was already named in the code name system.

Prior to this, three Messerschmitt Bf 109Es had been imported into Japan. Expecting to encounter these German designed fighters with Japanese pilots, the Messerschmitt was given the name **Mike** by Williams, thought to be a good nickname for the Messerschmitt. **Mike** happened to be the namesake of Master Sergeant Meyer "Mike" Levin, Colin Kelly's bombardier and a close friend of Williams. It was Kelly and his crew that were America's first war heroes when on December 10, 1941, it was reported that they had sunk the Japanese Battleship *Haruna* under very adverse conditions. The actual happenings were later learned to be quite different, but during this episode Kelly's B-17D was attacked by **Zekes** when returning to Clark Field in the Philippines. Kelly continued to control the damaged bomber while his crew, including Mike Levin bailed out near their home base, but Kelly failed to make it out. Levin was later assigned to the 43rd Bomb Group in New Guinea with B-17s in which he was shot down near Rabaul, New Britain.

Irving became a permanently used code name. This too was one assigned by Williams for his friend Irving Schwartz, formerly from Brooklyn, New York. They had been assigned

Meyer "Mike" Levin was the source for naming the Messerschmitt Bf 109Es, MIKE, although only three were shipped to Japan and none produced there. A friend of Williams, "Mike" Levin had been war-hero Colin Kelly's bombardier when their B-17D was shot down.

to the same Keystone B-6 bomber crew in Panama around 1936, but had lost track of each other once they were separated by assignments to different locations. Fran attached this male's name to the Nakajima J1N1 Gekko when it was learned that it was to be a long-range escort fighter. The airplane failed in that capacity, and the Japanese Navy changed its mission to that of a reconnaissance-plane. Rightfully, the Gekko should now have a feminine name, but it was not changed. The mission of the airplane changed again, and this time to a very successful night fighter. The male name of **Irving** now stood correctly.

It was a hot day in Australia when the Douglas C-54 Skymaster arrived while carrying McCoy's good friend Colonel W.M. "Woody" Burgess, from his recent temporary duty in Headquarters AAF in Washington. Burgess was the Army Air Forces Deputy for A-2 (Intelligence), and a strong supporter for Frank McCoy's work in the intelligence system. As they walked together from the airplane, Frank learned that the Burgess' had a new daughter. If Frank knew a person at all, he soon knew a lot about them, and remembered. The conversation eventually shifted to Frank telling "Woody" Burgess about the sighting of a new four-engine Japanese bomber. There was grave concern as to the threat this would bring to the Allies. It would need a code name. Frank asked if the name of their new daughter Elizabeth could be applied to this airplane? Burgess was pleased at the thought, and **Liz** became the

This is an early aerial reconnaissance photograph of the Nakajima J1N1, designed as a twin-engine fighter. As such, it required a masculine name and was assigned that of IRVING. This airplane later became an exceptional night fighter.

The namesake for the name IRVING that was assigned to the J1N1, was that of Irving Schwartz. A close friend of Fran Williams, the two were stationed together in Panama in 1936 when this picture of Schwartz was taken while gagging-it-up with San Blas Indian Jewelry.

code name for the Nakajima G5N1 Shinzan. Fortunately for the Allies, only six of this marginally successful aircraft type were built, and the Japanese turned their efforts and resources to an improved design later called **Rita** which did not reach maturity before the war ended. It was Burgess, later a Brigadier General and assigned to the USAF Air Defense Command as General Whitehead's ACS/ Intelligence in Colorado Springs, Colorado, that discussed with McCoy in later years what led to creating the NATO code system of naming Soviet aircraft for the same reasons that were encountered in the Southwest Pacific.

And so the naming of Japanese aircraft continued. In the course of this process, some of the men in the Allied Air Forces asked that a Japanese fighter be named after them, or a bomber after their wife or sweetheart. There also were more official suggestions that new Japanese aircraft be named after some outstanding airmen. Some of these requests were honored in a number of cases. Since records were not kept to give intended origins of these names, those that are identified here by the men that named them can be expected to be the most complete and final written record of this naming system.

By September 1942, units that operated in the Southwest Pacific Theater were using these code names exclusively in connection with the intelligence fact sheets and silhouettes of Japanese airplanes. The South Pacific and India-Burma theaters soon employed this intelligence material for their use as well. McCoy began a series of cables to Washington and to the Air Ministry in London, requesting their adoption of the same or similar system of standardized identification. His involved, strange-sounding messages on one occasion aroused suspicion, and he was summoned before General MacArthur's chief of operations to explain them since he had to clear all messages. He listened – then said he still didn't understand all of it, but if George (Gen. G.C. Kenney) wants it this way, he would O.K. the transmission, trusting that the receivers would understand it!

In late December 1942, the code-name system had been adopted by all United States armed forces. Several months later the British Air Ministry gave its approval. The responsibilities of air intelligence continued to grow in the evaluation of enemy equipment and capability. By October 1944, the Technical Air Intelligence Units (TAIUs) were upgraded with separate T/O & E's (Tables of Organization and Equipment) and attached to Far East Air Forces. Other intelligence responsibilities were realigned as well, making the U.S. Army

TECHNICAL AIR INTELLIGENCE UNIT (Unofficial Insignia)

responsible for the war in Europe, while the Pacific would be that of the Navy. As a result, evaluations of Japanese aircraft and related intelligence matters that had been carried out at the joint Army-Navy Technical Air Intelligence Center at Wright Field, Dayton, Ohio, were shifted to Anacostia NAS, Washington, D.C. in the summer of 1944. It was here that the final authority for the assignment of code names was approved.

The management of the code naming system, however, remained at FEAF Headquarters within the Pacific theater. As new Japanese aircraft types were discovered, code names were assigned, then coordinated through Washington, London and India. By the time the war ended, 122 names of Japanese aircraft had been identified as having been applied to operational, obsolete, as well as unsuspected fictional types. The list of code names was never classified, but instead, through press and radio, they became everyday terms that prevail to this day in identifying Japanese aircraft of the Pacific War.

Chapter II
Code Named Japanese Aircraft Described

This listing of Japanese aircraft by their Allied air intelligence assigned code name, also contains its Official Designation (Long Title), and its Project Designation (Short Title) shown in parenthesis. Separate listings by Official and Project Designations are contained in this book for cross referencing.

Not contained in this coverage, but referred to in some of the Navy nomenclatures are *Shi numbers.* Shi, meaning Shisaku Seizo, or *Trial Manufacture,* were numbers assigned to new Navy design projects, having as their prefix number the year of Showa of the Japanese calendar. When the aircraft was accepted by the Navy this Shi-number was dropped and replaced by a Type designation. Some aircraft listed here, such as LIZ and RITA, were not developed to that extent and therefore must be identified by their Shisaku number.

The descriptions are not intended to fully describe these aircraft, but instead provide a brief background that relates to the naming and identity of the aircraft. Where aircraft have been confirmed as actual types, their official nomenclature is used and not that which was originally reported. (See CHAPTER IV, *From The Basics,* for those early identifiers.) For fictitious and unconfirmed aircraft types, the designation used in reports that list the aircraft is used since an official title is non-existant. A document that was very helpful in matching an aircraft to an existing type was *JAPANESE AIRCRAFT MANUAL,* O.N.I. 249 (Office of Naval Intelligence), corrected to June 25, 1943. This manual contains 3-view drawings of many aircraft described here which helps confirm their identity.

As the code naming system matured, variations by adding suffixes to the code names became necessary. As a modification or variation to the basic type designs were noted, Mk 2, Mk 3, etc. were added after the code name. Unless there was a Mk 2 variant, the Mk 1 was not used.

With the improvement of intelligence gathering as the war progressed, it was learned that the Japanese also used a suffix system to their own designation. For the Army, this was a Roman numeral added to both the Ki numbering system, as well as to the Official Designation.

The Navy's system when reflecting sub-types within Official Designations consisted of one, and later two digits to describe the "Model." The first digit referred to the airframe change number while the second digit reflected the engine change number. These Japanese suffix or Model numbers, therefore, replaced the Mk numbers and became add-ons to the Allied code names as announced in the October 1944 issue of *Recognition Journal.* Two examples of Army and Navy designations respectively are: **Dinah 3** for the Ki-46-III, and **Zeke 32** for the Navy Type 0 Carrier Fighter Model 32, A6M3. This usage as an attachment to the code name was generally an exception rather than the rule, leaving basic descriptions as code name only.

ABDUL
Mitsubishi Navy Type 97 Fighter
(Fictional)

With the fighter **Claude** already identified, logic would indicate that a retractable landing gear version would be the next step in development. An air intelligence 3-view of **Abdul** was clearly a cleaned-up version of **Claude**. This aircraft described in O.N.I. 249 was the same as in Jane's All The World Aircraft, 1940, yet it never existed. What did develop from Mitsubishi after **Claude,** however, was the A6M Zero or **Zeke**. Some post-war sources have indicated **Abdul** to be a cleaned-up version of the Nakajima Ki-27 **Nate**, but this is known to be incorrect. The possibility of **Abdul's** existence persisted, and the name and description was carried in Naval recognition manuals as late as February, 1943.

ADAM
Nakajima Navy Type 97 Seaplane Fighter
(Fictional)

Early in the code naming period, several airplanes were inadvertently fictional, **Adam** being one of them. In profile, there were strong similarities with that of the Kawanishi E8K1 single float reconnaissance seaplane which could account for this drawing composition. As a twin-float design, **Adam** was even produced in the plastic model aircraft recognition series. Perhaps if known that the outline of this aircraft was hypothetical by intelligence personnel, logic would have it that Japan may have an airplane similar to this type, since float designs were plentiful. **Adam** would then provide a base-line in spotting and reporting.

ADAM

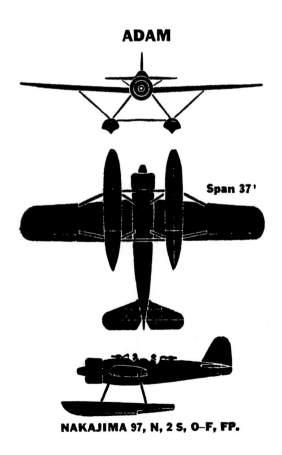

Span 37'

NAKAJIMA 97, N, 2 S, O–F, FP.

ALF
Kawanishi Navy Type 94 Reconnaissance Seaplane
(E7K)

This rugged but obsolete reconnaissance seaplane was used by the Japanese in China, then encountered in the Pacific War in the role of reconnaissance, anti-submarine patrol, and convoy escort until early 1943. Aside from **Dave**, its ultimate replacement was the E13A1 **Jake**. Having entered production in 1934, they soon were placed in service aboard warships when catapult-launched, seaplane tenders and shore bases for maritime reconnaissance. They had a variety of engines, beginning with a 500 hp Hiro Type 91 12-cylinder W liquid-cooled engine, and production ending with an 870 hp Mitsubishi Zuishi 11 14-cylinder radial engine. The name **Alf** applied to both the in-line and radial engine versions. Aircrews that operated these aircraft liked their ease of handling and reliability.

ANN
Mitsubishi Army Type 97 Light Bomber (Ki-30)

Ann served in many of the bomber units in China and was therefore widely publicized in the media, thus one of the early aircraft given a code name. Some were encountered in the early Philippine campaigns in support of the Japanese Army's occupation of the Philippines. It was soon after this operation in early 1942 that surviving aircraft of this type were relegated to training units. When under Japanese sponsorship in Indo-China, a few **Anns** were used by the Royal Thai Air Force against the French. Production reached just over 700 aircraft between 1937 and 1941. They were powered by one 850 hp Nakajima Army Type 97 14-cylinder radial air cooled engine. This fixed, faired landing gear and basic airframe design brought recognition confusion between a number of Japanese aircraft.

BABS
Mitsubishi Army Type 97 Command
Reconnaissance Plane (Ki-15)
Mitsubishi Navy Type 98 Reconnaissance Plane (C5M)

One of the better known pre-war Japanese aircraft was this fast reconnaissance type aircraft **Babs** that was designed for the Army and later used by the Navy as well. While in its early development period, the *Asahi Shimbun* acquired one of these aircraft as a civil aircraft that became known as Karigane I Communication Plane. It was given world acclaim with a goodwill flight from Tokyo to London in 1937. This proved its military value and thereafter production was increased for both services for the reconnaissance role. Soon outmoded by the very advanced Army Ki-46 **Dinah**, and Navy C6N **Myrt**, **Babs** were used heavily in China and Southeast Asia, but limited in the Pacific War. Versions of **Babs** varied by engine installations.

BAKA
Kugisho Navy Special Attacker Ohka

Departing from the gender code name system for this Navy kamikaze aircraft, the men on the receiving end of these attacks called this aircraft the "**Baka** Bomb," meaning *fool* in Japanese. With the development of this aircraft came an entirely new departure from conventional warfare whereby the pilot on their one-way flight to the target was expended for the cause of Japan. Being a tiny aircraft and with high speed in their final dive, the **Baka** Bomb was a difficult target to hit. They became operational in the Okinawan Campaign in the final months of the war, being carried to their target area beneath a **Betty** bomber. The Japanese name for the operational craft was *Ohka*, (cherry blossom), while those airframes used for flight testing and pilot training were MXY7 and MXY7-K1 respectively.

BELLE
Kawanishi Navy Type 90-2 Flying-boat (H3K1)

Another example of how little was known as to what to expect in the Pacific War, the Kawanishi H3K1 of the 1930 design period was already phased out of service by mid-1930s, yet given the code name **Belle**. Their design was based upon the Short Singapore and Calcutta built under license from Short Brothers of England. There were five of these flying boats in the Japanese Navy, built mostly from components purchased from England. Despite the publicity given to this design, Jane's All the World Aircraft of 1940 described these aircraft as Mitsubishi Type 96 Flying-boats. Each of these flying-boats had unique features in their configurations, however all were powered by three imported 825 hp Rolls-Royce Buzzard water-cooled engines. These aircraft established Kawanishi as the manufacturer of large flying-boats through the Pacific War.

BEN
Nagoya Sento-ki 001 Carrier Fighter

This is what evolved as being the Zero Fighter that was first encountered by Americans in the Pearl Harbor attack. Its identity came from the placard marking on one of the downed aircraft. Believing that the name Nagoya was the manufacturer, this was actually the location of the Mitsubishi plant. Sento-ki means fighter-type. Since the Zero Fighter was being encountered in other areas of the Pacific War, confusion developed in sorting out the identity of Japanese fighters. Following reports of this fighter, the name **Ben** was assigned, the namesake of Major Benjamin Cane. He was Frank McCoy's (the assigner of code names), immediate supervisor at that time. In less than a year, the name **Ben** was dropped when it was discovered to be a duplication of the fighter already code named **Zeke**.

Code Named Japanese Aircraft Described

BESS
Nakajima Type 98 Medium Bomber
Heinkel He 111

In the early stages of the Pacific War there were expectations of encountering German designed aircraft of many types. Any sign of interest in Japanese magazines of German aircraft brought speculation about their possible use. Code names were then assigned – just in case. The He 111 became **Bess**. Allied recognition listings carried **Bess** as a Nakajima Type 98 Medium bomber, and one source referred to it as a radial powered Aichi-built He 111 for the Army, although Aichi produced aircraft exclusively for the Navy. None were ever used by the Japanese nor an example imported into Japan.

BETTY
Mitsubishi Navy Type 1 Attack Bomber (G4M)
Mitsubishi Navy Type 1 Formation Escort Fighter (G6M1)
Mitsubishi Navy Type 1 Attack Bomber Trainer (G6M1-K)
Mitsubishi Type 1 Transport (G6M1-L2)

The name "**Betty Bomber**" became an overnight success in the Allied code naming system. It was named early because it was one of the first "new" types to be met in the Pacific War. The real Betty was a well proportioned nurse from Bridgewater, Pennsylvania, and friend of the one responsible for naming this airplane which had well defined blisters. These bombers were designed to support Naval operations from shore bases, relieving the fleet from having to support this form of air operations from aircraft carriers. **Bettys** operated throughout the entire Pacific War conflict as the mainstay of the Japanese Navy.

BOB
Aichi Navy Type 97 Reconnaissance Seaplane

In 1940, Jane's All the Worlds Aircraft used the Aichi nomenclature as stated above but without an illustration. When air intelligence assigned the code name **Bob** to this designation and description, a 3-view drawing was added, identified later as the Nakajima Navy Type 15 Reconnaissance Seaplane, E2N1 and 2, pictured here. This airplane was in Japanese Naval service from 1927 until replaced in the early 1930s by various models of Nakajima Type 90 reconnaissance seaplanes. Several of these earlier types remained in use by civil operators for air mail services and fish spotting as the "Nakajima Fishery Seaplane." This continued use may account for its known presence to the Allies because of magazine coverage, thus the need for having a code name.

BUZZARD
Kokusai Army Experimental Transport Glider
Manazuru (Ku-7)

Names of birds were assigned to Japanese gliders when their need for code names became apparent. Given the name **Buzzard**, this glider was to carry one tank or 32 fully armed troops into combat. The design began in 1942 when Japan was on the offensive. When the first flight took place in August 1944, the tide of war had changed in disfavor of Japan. New concepts were investigated, and the glider design was changed to a twin-engine assault transport as the Ki-105. These multi-purpose transports were also to be used as a fuel tanker to resupply fuel-starved Japan from resources in Sumatra. Nine prototypes were tested beginning in April 1945 of a plan calling for an ambitious 300 more of this type. When the war ended, 50 were in production. The name **Buzzard** also applied to this powered version.

CEDAR
Tachikawa Army Type 95-3 Primary Trainer (Ki-17)

Training aircraft were not included in the first listings of code named Japanese aircraft because they were not expected to be encountered in combat. As the war progressed, and Allied aircraft covered more of the once Japanese dominated skies, training aircraft were sure to be spotted in satellite countries of Japan as well as their home islands. It was appropriate that they too be given code names. Beginning in 1943 when the first trainers appeared on the aircraft recognition code lists, they were given names of trees to separate them as trainers. This Tachikawa Army primary trainer developed in 1935, was given the code name **Cedar**.

CHERRY
Kugisho Navy Type 99 Flying-boat (H5Y)

This airplane was known to air intelligence early in the war and was therefore listed among the first to be named. Given the name **Cherry**, twenty of these flying boats were built for Navy service between 1936 and 1941. They resembled a twin-engine version of the four-engine **Mavis** of which they were to supplement. However, these smaller aircraft were underpowered and saw limited service. Nevertheless, they were thought worthy of appearing on the Allie's non-operational list of Japanese aircraft for the SWPA (Southwest Pacific Area) as a means of identifying and monitoring these enemy aircraft.

CLARA
Tachikawa Army Experimental Command
Reconnaissance Plane
(Ki-70)

Intended to be a replacement for **Dinah**, only three of this type were actually built, the first being completed in February 1943. Its existence was learned through captured documents that listed a "Ki-70." The name of McCoy's mother-in-law, Clara, was assigned to the designation only, since illustrations of the aircraft were not seen until after the war. Performance of this aircraft hardly exceeded that for which it was to replace; **Dinah**, therefore, further attempts to develop **Clara** were abandoned.

CLAUDE
Mitsubishi Navy Type 96 Carrier Fighter (A5M)

The existence of this type aircraft was well known over China and at the beginning of the Pacific War. When given the name **Claude** on the first listing of Japanese code named aircraft, this carried the namesake of an Australian friend of McCoy's in Melbourne when the code names were being assigned. Before the Zero Fighter **Zeke** entered combat over China, Claude was the most feared fighter of the Japanese forces. Few saw combat in the Pacific War, for by this time most were relegated to the training-role. Because of the early widespread use of this Navy fighter, naming this airplane became duplicated with **Sandy**, a name that was soon dropped.

CLINT
Nakajima Type 97 Single Seat Fighter
(See **Nate**)

Found in an early undated Japanese Aircraft Manual published by US Naval Intelligence, **Clint** was obviously a name duplication for that of the **Nate** Army fighter. In the early encounters with Japanese aircraft, there was little concept of the number of aircraft types that Japan was using, therefore each sighting had to be judged on its merits until matched with an established type. The Army Type 97 fighter as **Nate** also carried the designation of Ki-27. This Army fighter was easily confused with the Navy's **Claude** of very similar configuration.

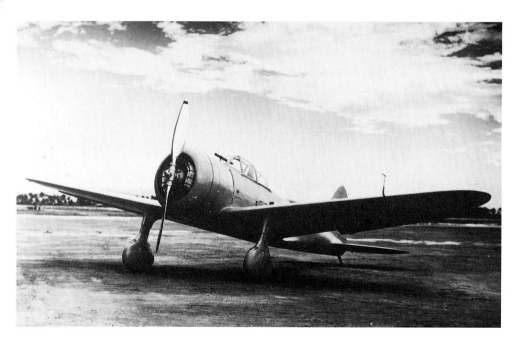

CYPRESS
Kyushu Navy Type 2 Primary Trainer Momiji (K9W1)
Kokusai Army Type 4 Primary Trainer (Ki-86)

One of few airplanes used by both services, **Cypress** was a license manufactured primary trainer of the German Bucker Bu 131B Jungmann. After a flight demonstration of this nimble two-seat biplane trainer in 1938, the Japanese Navy purchased twenty of these aircraft the following year. After obtaining a manufacturing license from Germany for the Bu 131B, Kyushu built 339 for the Navy, and Kokusai manufactured 1,037 for the Army. Only occasionally were they spotted during attacks over Japan. Named *Momiji* by the Japanese Navy which means *Maple*, Allied air intelligence would have done well to have used that tree name instead of their assigned code name **Cypress** for this airplane.

DAVE
Nakajima Navy Type 95 Reconnaissance Seaplane
(E8N1)

Dave was within the early group of Japanese airplanes to receive a code name since it too was used in China and generally publicized. This airplane remained active throughout the Pacific War as a catapult-launched reconnaissance aircraft, taking up second-line duties late in the war. Their mission was primarily that of gun-fire spotting for the fleet when engaged in combat, and when required, to defend the fleet as a fighter against attacking fighters. The larger fleet-based reconnaissance float aircraft were designed for long range reconnaissance missions. The origin of this 1933 design stemmed from the Vought Corsair that influenced **Dave's** predecessor, the E4N2 Reconnaissance Seaplane.

DICK
Seversky Navy Type S Two-seat Fighter (A8V1)

Known by its export designation, 2PA-B3, twenty of these American-built Severskys were exported to Japan in 1937 for use by the Japanese Navy as escort fighters over China. With rumors that Mitsubishi or Kawasaki were producing the airplane as the Type 98 Two-seat Fighter, it was given the code name **Dick**, yet it was never encountered in the Pacific War. There was popular belief among Allied aircrews that Japan might produce any of the foreign aircraft acquired by that country and therefore code named several of them although never encountered. Actually, Japan produced only four foreign designs during the Pacific War period, all of which were under license manufacture. These were **Cypress**, **Tabby**, **Thelma**, and **Oak**.

DINAH
Mitsubishi Army Type 100 Command Recon. Plane
(Ki-46)
Mitsubishi Army Type 100 Tact. Pilot Trainer
(Ki-46-IIKAI)
Mitsubishi Army Type 100 Air Defense Fighter
(Ki-46-IIIKAI)

One of the high performance airplanes of the Japanese Army was this high-altitude, high-speed reconnaissance aircraft code named **Dinah**. First flown two years before the start of the Pacific War, satisfaction was not attained until a two-stage supercharged engine became available so as to attain the specified 325 kn airspeed. The **Dinah** proved very successful and was used throughout the war by the Army, and a few by the Navy. The later model had a well rounded nose replacing this stepped windshield design. Japanese Model Numbers became part of the code name designator, this Model III version, therefore, became the **Dinah 3**.

DOC
Type Bf 110 Messerschmitt Twin-engine Fighter

Imported designs from Germany were expected of the Japanese air forces throughout the Pacific War. Reports of Japanese twin-engine fighter-like airplanes led Allied intelligence to believe that the Messerschmitt Bf 110 could be expected. To be ready for such sightings, the code name **Doc** was assigned and prevailed until 1943. None were ever sent to Japan, however, in January 1943 one Messerschmitt Me 210A-1 was imported for flight evaluation and comparison with other Japanese aircraft. It was perhaps not detected by the Allies and therefore not specifically identified in the code name series. According to the system, it may well have become **Doc 2**.

DORIS
Medium Bomber (Short Nose)

Reported sightings that were not readily matched to known Japanese aircraft types were treated as a new aircraft. The obvious distinctive feature of this sighting was the apparent short nose. Possible aircraft that may have been seen were **Nick**, **Lily** and **Hickory**. Since no further reports were received that even came close to this configuration as once reported, the type was dropped by mid-war.

" DORIS "

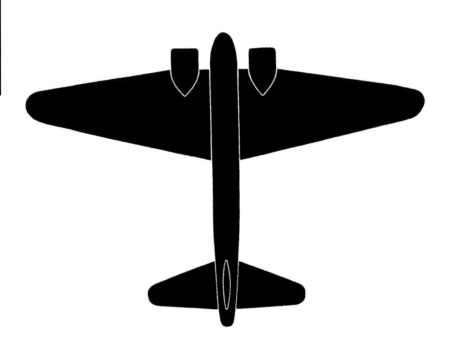

TYPE   M/B
Span 80′ Length 56′ Height

DOT
Nakajima Navy Type 1 Dive Bomber
(See JUDY)

Reports of new aircraft often led to confusion over mission type for that airplane. As a reconnaissance aircraft and soon followed by that of a carrier based bomber while still relatively new in combat explains why double naming of the same type occurred. The code name **Dot** was dropped when the airplane was discovered to be the already named **Judy**. Since Aichi built most of the **Judy** aircraft which at first was the Kugisho Navy Type 2 Carrier Reconnaissance Plane before assuming the dive bomber role, the Type 1 designation given to **Dot** remains unexplained.

EDNA
Manshu Army Experimental Tactical Reconnaissance/Assault Plane
(Ki-71)

Beginning in 1941, Manchurian Aeroplane Manufacturing Co. Ltd. redesigned the aging Ki-51 **Sonia** in an attempt to improve performance for this proven design. Designers gave the airplane a retractable landing gear and a 1,500 hp engine. This new engine was an improvement over the 950 hp engine that powered **Sonia**. Three prototypes were built but with disappointing improvement in performance. Although further development was discontinued, American intelligence learned of the new design early in the modernization program from prisoner interrogation. With this information they assigned the name **Edna**.

EMILY
Kawanishi Navy Type 2 Flying-boat (H8K)
Kawanishi Navy Transport Flying-boat Seiku (H8K2-L)

Only the Japanese knew that the bombs dropped in the vicinity of Honolulu the night of 4-5 March 1942 were from a Navy Type 2 Flying-boat. When met in aerial combat by Americans a few months later, it was described as having a slight gull wing, and illustrated as such. Code named **Emily**, they were soon sighted throughout the entire area of the Pacific where there was Japanese presence. As a replacement for the Kawanishi-built **Mavis**, they were often the only means of re-supply of the Japanese in many of the remote outreaches of the Pacific. They were heavily armed since their extreme range was beyond that of escorting fighters. This airplane proved to be the most effective 4-engine flying boat of the Pacific War.

EVE
Mitsubishi Ohtori Civil Long-range Communications Plane

Early reports of this aircraft listed it as a Nakajima Type 96 Army Twin-engine Medium Bomber. Reported in O.N.I. 247, it's crude 3-view drawing showed inset fins and long greenhouse that resembled more than any other aircraft the Mitsubishi *Ohtori* (Phoenix) Communications Plane. Linking the description to a photograph, the airplane was the *Ohtori* owned and operated by the *Asahi Shimbun* newspaper. This one of a kind airplane happened to be a Mitsubishi Army Type 93-2 Twin-engine Light Bomber **Louise** converted in 1936 for civil duty. The absence of protruding armament gave the airplane a more modern appearance with refined lines. Since the general bomber lines remained, it was listed as a bomber in recognition material and given the name **Eve** in anticipation of meeting this type in combat.

FRANCES
Kugisho Navy Bomber Ginga (P1Y)
Kugisho Navy Night Fighter Byakko (P1Y1-S)
Kugisho Navy Night Fighter Kyokko (P1Y2-S)

Thought to be a twin-engine fighter when first reported, this airplane was given the masculine code name of **Francis**. This was selected by the key "namer" of these airplanes, Francis "Fran" Williams. When the airplane was actually spotted sometime after its first flight that took place in August 1943, it was learned that it was a bomber. The name had to be changed to that of a feminine gender; **Frances**. This airplane was a marked contrast to that of earlier Japanese bombers, particularly those of the Navy. Instead of the usual multi-gun positions in these bombers, **Frances** utilized only one forward firing and one rear firing flexible gun for this crew of three, relying heavily upon speed for defense.

FRANK
Nakajima Army Type 4 Fighter Hayate (Ki-84)
(See **HARRY**)

Wishing to have his namesake on an active fighter, then Major Frank McCoy, head of the intelligence unit that was assigning these names, had his name reassigned to this fighter. The name **Frank** had been assigned at the outset of naming aircraft to the Mitsubishi T.K.4 Type O Special Fighter, which turned out to be a fictitious airplane (and later re-named **Harry**). It was obvious that this new fighter that now carried the name **Frank** was a certainty in the Japanese Army inventory of fighters. The Nakajima Ki-84 Hayate **Frank** was the Army's best fighter, entering operational service in late 1943. They were highly respected by any Allied pilot that engaged these aircraft to the very end of the war.

FRED
Focke-Wulf Fw 190 A-5

Expecting to meet Fw 190s flown by Japanese in the Pacific War, the name **Fred** was assigned in 1942 to this airplane. By the time the one and only Fw 190A-5 was sent to Japan in 1943, the code name was already in place albeit prematurely. This airplane was only planned to be used for evaluation by the Japanese for determining the progress being made by their own designs. With **Fred** and other German aircraft such as the Bf 109 **Mike**, Bf 110 **Doc** and He 111 **Bess**, it is interesting that these names never carried over into the European Theater of operation as code names for these same aircraft.

GANDER
Kokusai Army Type 4 Special Transport Glider (Ku-8)
(See **GOOSE**)

With code names of birds being applied to Japanese gliders, it was appropriate that **Gander**, being a large bird, was suited for this large glider. Initially the name **Goose** was used, but it was replaced with **Gander** when it was realized that this would be confused with the American Grumman JRF Goose amphibians which were also in the Pacific Theater. The design of this glider began in December 1941. It became the only Japanese transport glider to be met in combat, having as its only counterpart, the Kokusai Ku-7 **Buzzard**. Normally towed behind a Mitsubishi Ki-21 **Sally**, it could carry up to 20 soldiers or a small cannon with crew. Like the U.S. Army's Waco CG-4A, the nose hinged upward for front-end loading and unloading.

GEORGE
Kawanishi Navy Interceptor Fighter Shiden/Shiden Kai
(N1K1-J/N1K2-J)

When captured documents revealed that the float fighter **Rex** was being converted to a land-based fighter, Flight Sergeant George Remmington, RAAF, had his name applied to the N1K1-J Shiden. Remmington was assigned to this intelligence unit and made many of the silhouette drawings of Japanese airplanes for recognition purposes. The **George** had many problems in its development period which began in December 1942. They did not enter combat until the Allied invasion of the Philippines, and even then they were in relatively small supply. When pitted against the best of the Allied fighters of all services, **George** was found to be an able match for them all.

GLEN
Kugisho Navy Type 0 Small Reconnaissance Seaplane
(E14Y)

When the war began, little information was available about submarine-based aircraft of the Japanese Navy. The divulged designation; Type 0 Submarine-borne Aircraft identified one of these airplanes, and the name **Glen** was assigned to the Type before knowing what its appearance might be. Ten days after the Pearl Harbor attack, one of these **Glen** aircraft, launched from a submarine, surveyed the damage caused by that surprise attack. Later, a **Glen** was launched off the West Coast of the United States on a pre-dawn mission and dropped bombs in wooded territory in Oregon. Other missions by **Glens** were flown over Allied bases in Australia, New Zealand, Madagascar, the Aleutians, and East Africa.

GOOSE
Kokusai Army Type 4 Special Transport Glider (Ku-8)
(See **GANDER**)

This was a logical bird name for this large glider. Its use was soon discontinued, however, because of the name confusion it would have with the US Grumman JRF/OA-9 Goose amphibian which also operated in the Pacific. It was given the name **Gander** instead. Although smaller than the U.S. Army's Waco CG-4A assault glider, there were considerable similarities including the nose that hinged upward for discharging its cargo after landing. This was the only Japanese glider that was encountered in combat.

GRACE
Aichi Navy Carrier Attack Bomber Ryusei (B7A1)

When first spotted from the air and photographed while on the ground, its identity was linked to captured documents describing the type, and therefore, given the code name **Grace**. This was to be a replacement airplane for the carrier-based torpedo bomber **Jill**, but by now, Japan was without aircraft carriers. This was an exceptionally large aircraft for the intended Japanese carriers, yet it was in the same class with the Grumman TBF Avenger. Speed, range and weight carrying capability of **Grace** exceeded that of the Avenger. Appearing late in the war, production was hampered by an earthquake in May 1945, therefore **Grace** saw limited action in the Pacific War.

GUS
Nakajima Type AT27 Twin-engine Single-seat Fighter
(Fictional)

This was an advanced concept of a twin-tandem engine fighter having two counterrotating propellers and its two engines fore and aft of the cockpit. It could have been a military threat to the Allies if it existed, but it was a young designer's dream published in a pre-war Japanese magazine, and then misrepresented in the Western Press as an actual aircraft. The existence of **Gus** remained an uncertainty and was finally dropped from air intelligence listings in June 1943.

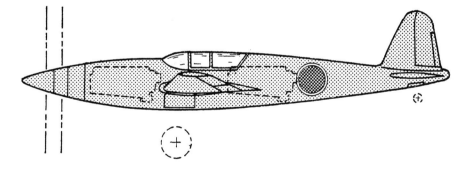

GWEN
Mitsubishi Type 0 Medium Bomber
(See **SALLY** and **JANE**)

Identified in the initial code name lists in the non-operational category and retained well into the war, **Gwen** may well have been the Ki-21-IIb, a later model of **Sally** which had dispensed with the earlier distinguishing feature of the long greenhouse replaced with a turret. Eventually realizing that both were the Ki-21 bomber, the name **Gwen** was dropped and the later model became **Sally Mk 3**.

HAMP
Mitsubishi Navy Type 0 Carrier Fighter Model 32
(A6M3)
(Also HAP)

When first spotted by the Allies in the Solomons area in late spring 1942, this clipped wing version of the Zero Fighter was thought to be a new design. It was given the name **Hap** in honor of General H.H. "Hap" Arnold, Commanding General of the AAF. His appreciation over the use of his name was questionable, thus, it was officially said that **Hap** was confusing with the word "Jap" and therefore changed to **Hamp**. When learned that the fighter was a modified Zero, **Hamp** was dropped in favor of **Zeke 32**. This is a good example of the Allied use of the Japanese applied model number in conjunction with the Allied nickname for a given airplane. Models of the **Zeke** that followed reverted back to the round wing tip.

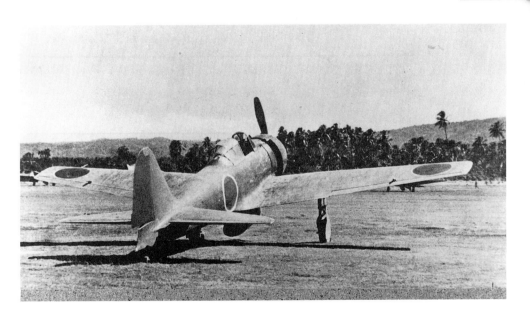

HANK
Aichi Navy Type 96 Reconnaissance Seaplane (E10A1)

For **Hank**, there was confusion with similarities. One month before the mention of **Hank** in code listings, **Laura** had appeared on the records as a Type 98 Flying Boat. When air intelligence learned of a "Type 98 Reconnaissance *Float Plane*," they clearly expected to find a "seaplane" to which they assigned the name **Hank**. However, both airplanes were quite similar, and therefore thought to be the same airplane for sometime. The two were finally sorted out, including the correction of Type 98 to Type 96 for the E10A1 flying boat configured **Hank**. The reason for the disparity in designation was that **Hank** was designed to meet specifications that described a seaplane in general terms, not specifying twin-floats or flying boat configuration. All 15 **Hank** aircraft were out of service before the Pacific War but it stayed on the recognition list until 1943.

HARRY
Mitsubishi Army Type 0 Single-seat Twin-engine Fighter
(Fictional)

Although not illustrated in O.N.I. 249, **Harry** was described as a design based on the Fokker D.XXIII with two B.M.W. 750 hp imported engines, subsequently to be redesigned to have two 1,000 hp Mitsubishi Kinsei air cooled radials. Originally it was named **Frank**, the namesake of McCoy who was in charge of the code naming project. When still waiting for its appearance, McCoy removed his name for that of a new aircraft coming into service, that being the Nakajima Ki-84 Hayate. To keep the Type 0 twin-engine fighter on the books as a possibility, it was given the first name of Col. Harry Cunningham, A-2 in New Guinea and friend of McCoy's.

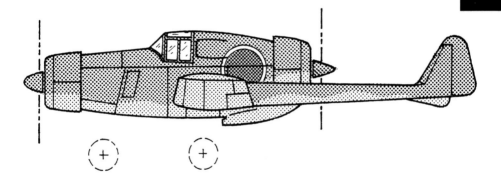

HELEN
Nakajima Army Type 100 Heavy Bomber Donryu
(Ki-49)

The existence of this bomber did not appear in air intelligence documents until September 1942 although they had been in service in China sometime before. This was the beginning of a new generation of bombers to appear after the start of the Pacific War. Intended as a replacement of **Sally**, **Helen** merely supplemented them. These were a much better protected bomber than its predecessors, but this added weight placed its bomb load and flight performance close to its under-protected predecessor **Sally**. Their presence was first observed in battles over New Britain and New Guinea, and most noted for their operations in the Philippines. As that battle turned in disfavor of the Japanese, many of the surviving **Helens** there were committed to kamikaze attacks.

HICKORY
Tachikawa Army Type 1 Advanced Trainer (Ki-54a)
Tachikawa Army Type 1 Operations Trainer (Ki-54b)
Tachikawa Army Type 1 Transport (Ki-54c)

As the war drew closer to the home islands, lesser types such as trainers would be expected to be seen, thus the naming of trainers as well. **Hickory** not only served as an advanced trainer, but as an operations (crew) trainer and light transport that could seat eight in the cabin. Some served Japanese forces in China as well. **Hickory** entered service as an advanced trainer in 1941 and served its many functions until the end of the Pacific War. The U.S. counterpart to this aircraft, both in size and type of missions flown was the eight passenger Beechcraft SNB, C-45, AT-7, and other variants. Several **Hickorys** survived to serve in the post war "Green Flight" air service with Japanese pilots for the few months of this operation.

IDA
Tachikawa Army Type 98 Direct Co-operation Plane (Ki-36)
Tachikawa Army Type 99 Advanced Trainer (Ki-55)

Identified as a Mitsubishi-built aircraft in early recognition material brought confusion with other fixed landing gear Japanese airplanes. It was eventually learned to be a light support bomber and reconnaissance airplane for the Army, and later produced as trainers. This namesake **Ida** which was used for both versions, was that of the fiance of Joe Grattan, code-naming team member. The airplane entered service in 1939 as a Direct Co-operation Plane, of which aircraft of this design were soon to be obsolete. Most were therefore relegated to operations in China where they encountered fewer Allied aircraft. As an advanced trainer Ki-55, **Ida** was very similar to the North American AT-6/SNJ Texan.

IONE
Aichi Navy Type 98 Bomber Float Plane
(Fictional)

With the heavy use of float planes by the Japanese, it was logical to assume that this airplane pictured in a pre-war Japanese magazine could be a Japanese design. In actuality, it closely resembles the Italian CANT Z.506B and was perhaps sketched from that design. When entered into the recognition manuals, it was named **Ione** after Ione Belvin, wife of Major Charles H. Belvin, an engineer and friend of McCoy's while stationed in Australia. Depicted as a three-engine aircraft as was the CANT Z.506B, there were no tri-motored aircraft in the Japanese inventories during the Pacific War. **Ione** remained on the recognition listings until early 1943 as a reconnaissance bomber and torpedo plane.

IRENE
Junkers Ju 87A Stuka

Japanese designers had a great respect for German-designed dive bombers. The Navy investigated several of these designs by importing latest examples for testing. When an example of a Ju 87A was brought into Japan by the Army in 1940, it was easy to assume that Japan would produce the Stuka and therefore gave it the code name **Irene**. What may have been learned from testing this aircraft has not been identified in the design of other aircraft. External wing dive brakes on the Japanese Navy's **Val** may have been influenced by the Stuka. Eventually, the Stuka was placed in the hangar-museum at Tokorozawa but was destroyed with many other notable aircraft when an Allied air raid was made upon that airfield near Tokyo.

IRVING
Nakajima Navy Type 2 Land Based Recon. Plane (J1N1-C)
Nakajima Navy Type 2 Gekko (Night Fighter) (J1N1-S)

When the Allies first learned of this aircraft, it was to be an escort fighter. The name **Irving**, a male name for fighters was appropriately applied. This twin-engine fighter was nicknamed **Irving**, after Irving Schwartz formerly from Brooklyn, N.Y., close friend of Fran Williams, code-naming team member. When proven unsatisfactory as a fighter, existing airframes of **Irving** were converted to the reconnaissance role instead. Fortunately its male name was not exchanged for a female name as applied to reconnaissance aircraft, but instead, the airplane later developed into an exceptional night fighter. It was the first Japanese aircraft to incorporate oblique dorsal and ventral mounted guns for attacks against bombers from below and above.

JACK
Mitsubishi Navy Interceptor Fighter Raiden (J2M)

Jack was named before this type ever saw combat. Because of the lengthy period of development, time permitted the leak of information about the airplane through captured data. By the time **Jack** was in action in the Philippines, the Allied Forces were familiar with its appearance, already coupled to a code name. Although created by the designer of **Zeke** and from the same company, the mission of **Jack** differed by being a land based interceptor with a high rate of climb to protect Japan's cities and airfields. Although conceived soon after **Zeke**, it was slow in reaching production because of engine development problems. When **Jack** entered combat in late 1943 in small numbers, they were a formidable fighter for Allied pilots to deal with.

JAKE
Aichi Navy Type 0 Reconnaissance Seaplane (E13A)

At first, **Jake** was thought to be a seaplane version of **Val**, and therefore a bomber. In that regard it was given a feminine name for bombers as **June**. When it was later discovered that this was a reconnaissance seaplane, it was given the masculine name of **Jake**. Before long, the duplication was discovered, the name of **June** was dropped. The similarities between **Jake** and **Val** were understandable since both came from the Aichi Aircraft Company and **Jake** came but one year later. These reconnaissance seaplanes appeared in combat starting in late 1941, and spearheaded the attack on Pearl Harbor. In addition to strategic reconnaissance duties, they were sometimes used for bombing missions whenever Allied air opposition was limited. Endurance missions of fifteen hours were not uncommon for this airplane.

JANE
Mitsubishi Army Type 97 Heavy Bomber (Ki-21)
(See **SALLY** and **GWEN**)

J
A
N
E

In the early months of the Pacific War the sighting of any Japanese airplane made identification a major challenge. There were many similarities and several modifications within these types. As a result and often when in doubt, a new name was assigned when thought to be a new aircraft. **Jane** was one of these duplications in assigning this name to the **Sally** bomber. When the duplication was discovered, the name **Sally** was retained.

JANICE
Type Junkers Ju 88 Army Twin-engine Medium Bomber

Air intelligence learned that Japan had imported one model of the Junkers Ju 88A-4 in 1940. It seemed plausible that this type may be manufactured in Japan and therefore eventually met in combat. Given the name **Janice**, it appeared in the initial code name listings and lasted to mid-war. No others were imported nor manufactured. Like that of other imported aircraft, Japan may have only intended to evaluate this German attacker when it was new, with no thought of manufacturing plans.

JEAN
Kugisho Navy Type 96 Carrier Attack Bomber (B4Y)

This type was known to the Allies before the war and was thought to be the torpedo bomber that would be met in any attacks made by Japan. Since **Kates** were revealed at Pearl Harbor, this biplane carrier bomber was classed as a second line aircraft by air intelligence, yet warranted having a code name. Given the name **Jean** on the early code name listings, it was named after the wife of General Douglas MacArthur. None were ever encountered by Allied crews during the Pacific War, and the few that remained were relegated to the training role for the Japanese Navy.

JERRY
Heinkel Navy Type He Intercepter Fighter (A7Hel)
Heinkel He 112B-0

A squadron strength numbering 30 He 112B fighters was purchased by Japan in 1938. Many complications can be imagined for maintaining an advanced combat aircraft in far off China. Unaccustomed to maintaining liquid cooled in-line engines of this type further complicated matters for the Japanese. Allied air intelligence knew of their use by the Japanese Navy, and gave them the code name **Jerry**. None were ever encountered by Allied forces and they were probably already out of service in China by the time the Pacific War began. As a result, the name **Jerry** lasted but a short time for Japanese aircraft nicknames. They provided much propaganda for Japanese forces. Striking unit markings emblazoned their fuselage sides, differing on the opposite side to imply greater numbers in strength when photographed.

JILL
Nakajima Navy Carrier Attack Bomber Tenzan (B6N)

This aircraft code named **Jill**, did not appear in combat as a replacement for the **Kate** torpedo bomber until the battle off the Marianas. Its existence was learned long before that battle by Allied air intelligence because of its long development period of nearly three years. In anticipation of its appearance, the code name **Jill** was assigned to this three man carrier-based bomber. This could have been a far more effective bomber and torpedo carrier had it been flown by better trained crews. As it was, appearing late in the war, skilled pilot resources were limited. They were widely used in attacks against American carriers and other surface ships particularly in battles around Okinawa in conventional and kamikaze attacks.

JIM
Kawasaki Type 1 Single-seat Fighter
(See OSCAR)

Since Japan was on war fronts over a very broad area, duplication in assigning code names was inevitable. When an airplane was reported as a Type 1 fighter with retractable landing gear, it was given the name of **Jim**. This identity eventually revealed that this was the previously named Nakajima Army Type 1 Fighter named **Oscar** and the name **Jim** and the erroneous Kawasaki built fighter designation was dropped.

JOAN
Type 99 Four-engine Flying-boat

There are two points that may have caused errors in reporting this airplane that was given the nickname **Joan**. The actual Type 99 Flying-boat was not four-engined, but only twin-engined and was code named **Cherry**. As for the four-engined identity, the upgrading of the Type 97 four-engine Transport Flying-boat **Mavis** to that of a patrol bomber with some external feature changes may account for what was thought to be a new aircraft. This is speculation, but a Type 99 Four-engine Flying-boat never existed, and therefore the aircraft described by the code name **Joan** never existed. The aircraft pictured here is **Mavis**, and thought to be the aircraft sighted and reported as a different aircraft.

JOE
Type T.K.19 Single-seat Fighter
(Fictional)

Corporal Joe Grattan was one of the three team members that were responsible for the code naming of Japanese airplanes. When this T.K.19 was found illustrated in a pre-war Japanese magazine, his name of **Joe** was assigned, thinking that this would be an aircraft soon to be engaged in combat. Like some of the others, this was a "dream airplane" never again repeated except in Allied air intelligence material. The error was soon discovered and the name and description was dropped from Japanese aircraft listings.

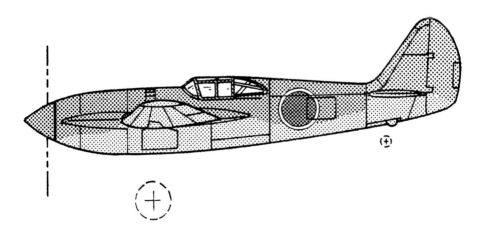

JOHN
Type 2 Fighter
(See **Tojo**)

The entry for this aircraft appeared in Air Headquarters, India, *Weekly Intelligence Summary* dated 21 November 1943. Later listings deleted the name **John** but carried **Tojo** in its place. Assuming that Type 2 is correct when reporting this seemingly new aircraft, and because of the area in which it was reported, it would logically be an Army aircraft, thus **John** could have been a duplication in naming the Nakajima Army Type 2 Single-seat Fighter, Ki-44 **Tojo**. For unknown reasons, the nickname **Tojo** prevailed.

JOYCE
Nakajima Army Type 1 Light Bomber
(See EVE)

Described in O.N.I. 247 initially as a Nakajima Army Type 1 Twin-engined Medium Bomber, revisions changed this to a Type 1 Light Bomber similar to a "ME 110 type aircraft." Another reference included "ground attack." This leaves speculation that the often pictured twin-tailed Mitsubishi Ohtori was both **Joyce** and the erroneous bomber called **Eve**. Army WAAF Joyce Gillie, who was working with the intelligence team in Australia, had her name assigned to this newly reported bomber. When its true identity was learned or no further reports were made describing this airplane, the names **Joyce**, **Eve** and their designations were dropped from the aircraft recognition listings.

JUDY
Kugisho Navy Type 2 Carrier Reconnaissance Plane (D4Y1-C)
Kugisho Navy Carrier Bomber Suisei (D4Y)

When this airplane was under development and well before its appearance, it was known to be in two models; carrier reconnaissance and carrier bomber. Since female code names applied to both categories, the name **Judy** worked well when serving either mission. Initially, this aircraft was powered by the more pointed appearing Atsuta liquid-cooled in-line engine. Numerous problems with this engine caused later models to use the Kinsei air-cooled radial engine. Although this change altered the overall appearance, the name **Judy** held for both configurations, the latter version being known as **Judy 33**. The majority of this Navy (Kugisho) designed airplane was built by Aichi.

192

JULIA
Kawasaki Army Type 97 Medium Bomber

Jane's All the World Aircraft described an airplane by this nomenclature in their wartime editions beginning in 1940, but without an illustration. Other sources reported that an aircraft of this type had been spotted in China. Designations ranged from "OB-97 to "Kawa 97." The O.N.I. 247 specifications matched those carried by Jane's but added the silhouette shown here. When further sightings of this aircraft that was code named **Julia** failed to materialize, the earlier reports of this aircraft were thought to have been confused with the Kawasaki Ki-48 **Lily**. As a result, the name **Julia** and its description were eliminated from the Japanese aircraft listings.

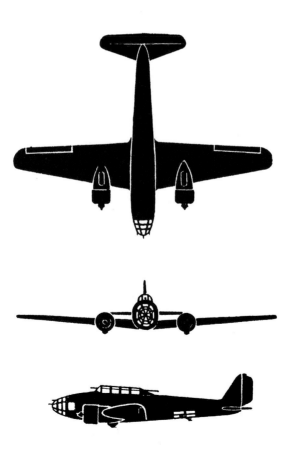

JUNE
Navy Type 99 Single Engine Dive Bomber Seaplane

The similarity in air frames between **Val** the dive bomber, and a new seaplane, led air intelligence personnel to believe that this was a float equipped **Val** dive bomber. As a bomber it was given the feminine name of **June**. When inspecting the first crashed aircraft of this type, it was revealed that this was an all new airplane. Recognizing that this was a reconnaissance float plane, it was given an appropriate masculine name, that of **Jake**.

" JUNE "

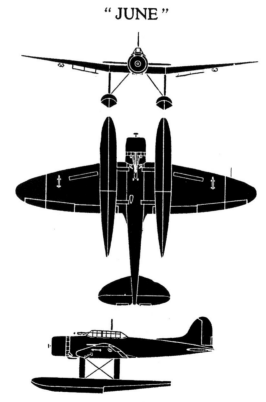

TYPE 99 DB F/P
Span 47' 7" Length 36' Height 13' (including Float)

NAVY

KATE
Nakajima Navy Type 97 Carrier Attack Bomber (B5N)

Having been in combat in China for three years before the Pacific War began, this airplane was not taken into account until it became known as the torpedo bomber used in the Pearl Harbor attack. It was a very modern aircraft by world standards at the time of this attack. Its existence was reported in Japanese magazines as a type being used in the war in China, but Western sources failed to recognize its presence. The first of this type to be studied was one that was recovered from the waters of Pearl Harbor. **Kate** became obsolete quickly in the Pacific War for lack of armor plate and fuel tank protection. Its replacement was that of **Jill**. Both carried their torpedoes externally.

LAURA
Aichi Navy Type 98 Reconnaissance Seaplane (E11A)

The existence of **Laura** was carried on the Allied list of Japanese aircraft as an "Aichi Type 98 Single-engine Flying-boat" from 1942, yet its appearance did not occur until after the Pacific War. In the interim there was confusion in differentiating this airplane over that of the very similar appearing **Hank**. Only seventeen **Laura's** were built, therefore they saw limited service. They were designed for catapulting from cruisers and battleships for night reconnaissance. The Japanese Navy took very seriously the aspect of night naval engagements, therefore designed this and other aircraft for the primary purpose of observing gunfire spotting at night for the purposes of making corrections. Since the Pacific War became primarily aerial engagements rather than surface, the effectiveness of night aerial observation for gun laying is seldom mentioned.

LILY
Kawasaki Army Type 99 Twin-engine Light Bomber
(Ki-48)

The twin-engine light bomber **Lily** was among the first Army bombers to be encountered in the Pacific War by the Allies. Against Chinese opposition, Japanese air crews reported very satisfactory performance, but when in combat against Allied fighters, they found that speed, defensive firepower and bomb load was sorely lacking. Although lacking many of the qualities of a good light bomber, **Lily** served the bomber forces of the Japanese Army in Northern China beginning in the autumn of 1940, continuing throughout the Pacific until nearly all were expended in the final engagements of the Okinawan campaign. Numerous design changes were attempted to improve performance, but basically, **Lily** remained unchanged throughout the war.

LIZ
Nakajima Navy Exp. 13-Shi Attack Bomber Shinzan
(G5N)

When the existence of this four-engine bomber was first spotted from the air, it was considered a dangerous threat. Col. W.M. "Woodie" Burgess, AAF Deputy A-2 was visiting the war zone from Washington at this time, and Lt. Col. Frank McCoy, whose unit was responsible for Japanese aircraft code names, recognized the visit by naming this bomber **Liz** after the Col's. newly born daughter Elizabeth. The design of **Liz** was heavily influenced by the Douglas DC-4E four-engine airliner, of which Japan had purchased many of the drawings before the airliner was completed. **Liz** had many design drawbacks that also appeared in the airliner, and only six were built by 1941. Many tests and engine upgrades were made to no avail and plans for production changed to that of the later design **Rita**. **Liz** aircraft then served mostly as transports.

LORNA
Kyushu Navy Patrol Plane Tokai (Q1W)

One of the less glamorous Japanese airplanes was this Navy anti-submarine patrol aircraft for home defense that was given the name of **Lorna**. The war was coming to a conclusion in 1945 before one was spotted, yet its existence was known, based upon captured documents and therefore code named. This was Japan's first attempt at a specialized anti-submarine patrol aircraft, a need that became apparent as the war approached the Japanese islands. **Lorna** had the capability of attacking surface craft by level bombing as well as diving attacks. These aircraft were equipped with search radar as well as magnetic anomaly detection gear. In addition to operating from bases in Japan, **Lornas** were stationed on Formosa and in China to protect Japanese convoys bringing critical materials and oil from sources in the Southwest Pacific.

LOUISE
Mitsubishi Army Type 93-2 Twin-engined Light Bomber
(Ki-2-II)

Mis-identified early in the naming sequence as the Mitsubishi Type 98 Medium Bomber, **Louise** had many exterior differences over the earlier, non-code-named model that was known as the Ki-2-I. Anxious to include family names in the coding system, Frank McCoy named this Light Bomber, **Louise**, after his wife. Unknowingly, this type airplane had been removed from service well in advance of the opening attacks of the Pacific War. The origin of this bomber design that began in 1932 was heavily influenced by the one imported Swedish-built Junkers K 37, an aircraft that saw combat with the Japanese in Manchuria and proved superior to other Japanese bombers employed there.

LUKE
Mitsubishi Navy Exp. 17-Shi Otsu Type Interceptor Fighter
(J4M)

The prototype of this airplane was under construction when the program was cancelled in favor of the Kyushu J7W1 Shinden as an air defense interceptor. The existence of the twin-boom pusher fighter as a concept was known to U.S. air intelligence through captured documents. It was reported in the January 1945 *U.S. Recognition Journal*, yet not initially illustrated. In anticipation of being met one day in combat, it was described and code named **Luke**. Several post-war renderings have been created that depict **Luke**, all of which are speculative concepts created from written descriptions.

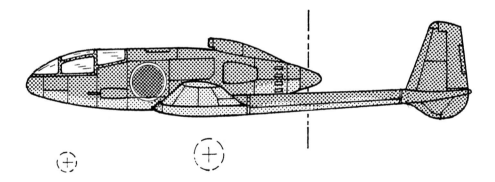

MABEL
Mitsubishi Navy Type 97-2 Carrier Attack Bomber
(B5M)

This airplane was designed and accepted under the same specifications as that of the Nakajima Type 97-1 which became **Kate**. The main physical differences between the two was that **Mabel** had a fixed landing gear. **Mabel** operated primarily in Southeast Asia and could have easily been confused with the dive bomber **Val**. The name **Mabel** that appeared on the second listing of code names was the namesake of a Mabel from the University of Oklahoma. She was a good friend of Frank McCoy, the person responsible for the code name system. Because of the similarity in mission specification and appearance between **Mabel** and that of the more widely seen **Kate**, the name **Mabel** was dropped in favor of **Kate 61**.

MAISIE
Medium Bomber

This is a case of assigning a code name to an unidentified medium bomber when descriptions from combat reports did not match aircraft with known identities. In time the confusion did clear because the airplane that the air intelligence system had code named **Maisie**, may have never been reported again, or that further reports coincided with an identified type, similar to **Nick** pictured here. Either circumstance would bring about the deletion of the code name **Maisie** and the airplane it described.

MARY
Kawasaki Army Type 98 Light Bomber (Ki-32)

Having a close similarity in appearance between this aircraft and the Mitsubishi Ki-30 **Ann**, the two were often confused when encountered over China. The code names which differentiated the various types helped solve some of this problem. The Kawasaki Ki-32 **Mary** differed primarily by having an in-line engine over that of the radial engined **Mary**. None of these 1937 vintage **Mary** aircraft were reported operational in the Pacific War, but were confined to units in mainland China and training duties in Japan. Some were instrumental in bringing about the surrender of the Commonwealth forces defending Hong Kong at the outset of the war. Engine development problems gave **Mary** a slow start in production but eventually outnumbered **Ann** by nearly 200 machines.

MAVIS
Kawanishi Navy Type 97 Flying-boat (H6K)

With a close similarity in design to that of the Sikorsky S-42 Pan American flying-boat, this Type 97 Flying-boat was the largest aircraft of Japan when the war began. It served in substantial numbers as a civil transport as well as a patrol reconnaissance bomber for the Japanese Navy. As a result of its high visibility in pre-war aviation magazines, **Mavis** was on the first list of code names assigned. These large flying-boats connected the far reaches of the Japanese empire and therefore were frequently encountered in the opening phase of the Pacific War. They were highly vulnerable to any fighter attacks. Military versions had numerous defensive gun positions but were still no match for Allied fighters. The few that survived were supplemented by the more advanced Kawanishi **Emily** patrol bomber.

MIKE
Messerschmitt Bf 109 E-3

In May 1941, three Bf 109Es were purchased by the Japanese Army for evaluation purposes. Since this fighter was lauded as the best in the European war, the JAAF wanted to flight test their Ki-43, Ki-44, Ki-60 and Ki-61 against the Bf 109E. Allied intelligence, however, interpreted their acquisition as pre-production models for the Japanese and anticipated that Bf 109Fs may be encountered with Japanese pilots. In preparation for this, air intelligence assigned the code name **Mike** to the Messerschmitts. None were ever manufactured in Japan, nor were these evaluation aircraft flown in combat although occasionally, erroneously reported in early aerial encounters with the Japanese.

MILLIE
Type 98 Showa Light Bomber
(Vultee V-11GB)

Manufacturing rights were allegedly sold by the American firm, Vultee Aircraft, to Japan for building their V-11GB Attack Bomber. This action brought considerable criticism to the company because of the pending 1938 embargo against Japan. None were ever imported, nor were attempts made to build the airplane in Japan. The Showa name pertains to the time era of Japan, not the Showa Aircraft Company that was not formed until 1939.

MYRT
Nakajima Navy Carrier Reconnaissance Plane Saiun
(C6N)

One of the best performing aircraft of all types built by the Japanese was what became code named **Myrt**. Its existence was known in advance by one of these aircraft being found in very poor condition by the Allies after the recapture of the Marianas. Because of their great speed and high altitude while performing reconnaissance missions, few were shot down over their target areas. As a carrier-borne reconnaissance airplane, the airframe was conducive to other missions such as being a torpedo bomber. With the loss of all aircraft carriers, this conversion was abandoned. In the defense of the home islands of Japan, and because of their outstanding performance, some **Myrts** were modified as night fighters with obliquely mounted cannon above and behind their canopy.

NATE
Nakajima Army Type 97 Fighter (Ki-27)

This was perhaps the best known pre-Pacific War Japanese fighter to Allied air intelligence because of the many published pictures. It was used extensively in China and frequently confused with its Navy counterpart code named **Claude**. Both were open cockpit fighters with fixed, panted landing gear. Because of the wide spread area of combat, the Type 97 Fighter was given the code name **Nate** in one area, and **Clint** in another. When the duplication was detected early in the code naming program, the singular name of **Nate** prevailed. **Nate** played a major role in the early war invasions of the Philippines, Malaya, Netherlands East Indies and Burma. The newer **Oscar** soon took the lead as the Army's front line fighter, and **Nate** was retained as a home defence fighter and trainer until fully phased out in 1943.

NELL
Mitsubishi Navy Type 96 Attack Bomber (G3M)

Nell was a well known Japanese aircraft long before the Pacific War and therefore given an early code name. The nickname **Nell** for this bomber was selected by Frank McCoy, recognizing the wife of his close friend Captain (later Col.) Ray W. McDuffey of 5th Air Force Intelligence at that time. Attacks by **Nells** in 1937 against mainland China from home bases in Japan made this the first transoceanic air attack in aerial warfare. In spite of the combat accomplishments of this Navy bomber, the world failed to fully realize the magnitude of threat that Japan had over the entire Pacific area. Although **Betty** became the replacement bomber for **Nell**, these older bombers were often met in combat by Allied crews well into 1943. There were many design features of this aircraft that were more advanced than with other Allied bombers at the time they entered Navy units in late 1936.

NICK
Kawasaki Army Type 2 Two-seat Fighter Toryu
(Ki-45KAI)

Although **Nick** entered combat in Burma and China in October and November 1942 respectively, it did not receive a code name until the following year. There was confusion at first over this aircraft because of possibly being a light bomber. **Nick** was basically a day fighter, following the trend in Europe and the United States in the development of twin-engine fighters. First-line units found **Nick** to be useful in a ground-attack and anti-shipping role because of the forward firing 37 mm cannon mounted in the ventral tunnel that was supplemented by a variety in number of nose mounted forward firing cannons. Many were modified late in the war to serve as night fighters for home defense by having obliquely mounted upward firing cannon behind the pilot seat.

NORM
Kawanishi Navy Type 2 High-speed Reconnaissance Seaplane Shiun (E15K)

Great expectations were held for this airplane by both the Japanese and the Allies. It was first revealed to the Allies in 1943 through captured Naval documents along with other Naval prototypes early in their development stages. Expecting to one day meet this aircraft in combat and therefore needing a code name, that name became **Norm**, in recognition of S/Ldr Norman Clappison, RAAF, a revered Australian team leader within the Technical Air Intelligence Unit. However, as this aircraft development continued, its counterrotating propellers and retractable wing tip floats proved too complex and a mere fifteen were produced by 1944. The more conventional and successful seaplane fighter **Rex**, also by Kawanishi, followed in the design path of **Norm** one year later.

NORMA
Mitsubishi Type 97 Light Bomber Darai 108

The airplane depicted here, as well as photographs used to illustrate the Type 97 Light Bomber, is the little publicized American-built Bennett all wood twin-engine airplane of 1938. Found illustrated in Japanese magazines, it was interpreted to be a Japanese light bomber. First listed as such in Allied recognition documents in September 1942, it was dropped the following June. How this nomenclature was ever assigned, as well as the meaning of the term Darai 108 remains unexplained.

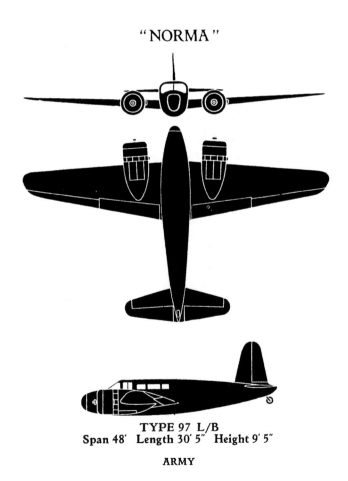

"NORMA"

TYPE 97 L/B
Span 48′ Length 30′ 5″ Height 9′ 5″

ARMY

OAK
Kyushu Navy Type 2 Intermediate Trainer (K10W)

Since North American Aviation had sold two NA-16 trainers to Japan along with manufacturing rights in 1937, it was only natural that air intelligence would be expecting to see aircraft of this design in Japanese service. Because of this, the code name **Oak** was assigned. The Japanese Navy made considerable design changes to this intermediate trainer, particularly in the tail section before awarding the production contract to Watanabe, later named Kyushu. After twenty-six aircraft were built, their manufacture was then moved to Nippon Aircraft Company for an additional 150 aircraft by 1944.

OMAR
Sukukaze 20, Twin-engine Single-seat Fighter
(Fictional)

Not realized by Allied air intelligence, this airplane they code named **Omar** was a fictitious design. It was pictured with what became **Gus, Harry** and **Joe** in an April 1941 Japanese magazine, all of which were believable designs at the time. If **Omar** were in actuality, it boasted a 400 mph speed provided by two engines in tandem. Literal translation of *Sukukaze*, is *Cool Breeze*. It must be remembered that at the time that the Allied Technical Air Intelligence Unit was developing a listing of Japanese aircraft, only fragmentary information often gleaned from pre-war Japanese magazines is all that was available. Establishing this base line of information was bound to contain errors initially.

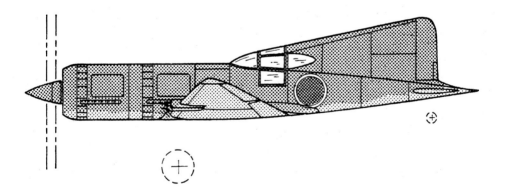

OSCAR
Nakajima Army Type 1 Fighter Hayabusa (Ki-43)

Mistaken in the air by some as a Zero, this Army fighter code named **Oscar** used a nearly identical engine as the Zero, but the airplane lacked the performance of the Zero. Instant recognition in aerial combat between **Oscar** and the Zero, code named **Zeke** was essential in the choice of combat technique. Early reports referred to this being a **Nate** with retractable landing gear. Known more popularly to the Japanese as Hayabusa, **Oscar** was the most important airplane to the Japanese Army in terms of quantity in service. They flew on every front to which the Army was committed. When reported as an unknown fighter in the China-Burma-India theater, it was given the code name of **Jim**. When learned that this was a duplication of the same airplane, **Oscar** prevailed. Although replaced by later types toward the end of the war, **Oscars** served continually to the very end.

PATSY
Tachikawa Army Experimental Long-range Bomber
(Ki-74)

Early information concerning new Japanese airplanes led air intelligence to believe that the reported Ki-74 was a single seat fighter. As such they assigned the masculine name of **Pat**. It was later learned that the Ki-74 was a long-range high-altitude reconnaissance-bomber, therefore feminizing the name to **Patsy** as announced in May 1945. To help achieve its mission of reaching select targets in the United States, **Patsy** had a pressurized cabin for all five crew members in the forward compartment. Changes to this plan as the situation for Japan continued to deteriorate called for bombing attacks against B-29 bases as soon as sufficient numbers of **Patsy** were available. The war ended before any aircraft of this type were met in combat.

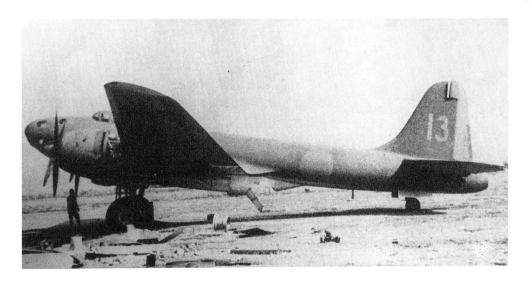

PAUL
Aichi Navy Reconnaissance Seaplane Zuiun (E16A)

By mid to late in the war, air intelligence had improved to the point that new airplanes were known before seen in combat. In the case of this reconnaissance seaplane, it was known of in advance, including drawings of the prototype aircraft. The name **Paul** was assigned. This two-place aircraft was under development only one year after its predecessor, Aichi's three-place E13A long-range reconnaissance seaplane named **Jake**. This newer airplane, however, had an added mission of being a dive bomber. They were fitted with slotted dive brakes extending from the front float-pylon. By the time **Paul** entered service during the 1944 Philippine campaign, Japanese air superiority had been lost, and thus their effectiveness. Most were then expended in suicide attacks in the Okinawan campaign.

PEGGY
Mitsubishi Army Type 4 Heavy Bomber Hiryu (Ki-67)
Mitsubishi Army Type 4 Special Attack Plane
(Ki-67-IKAI)

Arriving in combat late in the war, this airplane compared favorably with contemporary Allied twin-engine bombers and was the Japanese Army's best. As such, it was also flown by the Navy in small numbers which they named it *Yasukuni*. Code named **Peggy**, they were used initially in torpedo attacks off Formosa in October 1944. These bombers also operated in China as well as from Japan, using Iwo Jima as a staging base when making attacks against Marianas B-29 air bases. **Peggy** appeared in several configurations, one being redesignated as the Ki-109, serving as a high altitude destroyer of B-29s by carrying a 75 mm cannon in its nose to stay out of defensive fire of the B-29. Another version was that of a kamikaze aircraft with a large explosive charge built inside to detonate on impact.

PERRY
Kawasaki Army Type 95 Fighter (Ki-10)

Identified at first in recognition documents as the Kawasaki Type 98 single-seat fighter, it was given the name **Perry** in anticipation that this biplane would be met in combat. Actually, the airplane was three years older than the "Type 98" designation implied, and was already relegated to advanced fighter training units. At the beginning of the Pacific War it was thought by many that biplanes of this type would be the configuration of Japanese airplanes met in combat. Pre-war aviation magazine coverage showed **Perry** as a first line Japanese Army fighter, but by the start of the war, the **Nate** that replaced **Perry** was already being replaced by the much later **Oscar**.

PETE
Mitsubishi Navy Type 0 Observation Seaplane (F1M)

While most Japanese seaplanes served the Navy's mission as long-range reconnaissance aircraft, this airplane code named **Pete** was in a designation class by itself. Its mission while serving aboard seaplane tenders and cruisers was primarily that of observation for spotting naval gunfire as well as having a fighter capability for protecting the fleet. Not only did it serve the role just described, but that of coastal patrol, convoy escort and dive-bomber if needed in support of amphibious operations. **Pete** was one of few combat biplanes in production, world wide, during the Pacific War. As a biplane, this was an extremely clean design with a well streamline-strutted center-line float with "I" strut wing fittings replacing the conventional "N" strut bracings.

Code Named Japanese Aircraft Described

PINE
Mitsubishi Navy Type 90 Operations Trainer (K3M)

This high-wing monoplane was an unusual configuration for an air crew trainer. It appeared antiquated for this purpose from the start, yet it remained in Naval service through all of the Pacific War period. Expecting to encounter some of these aircraft over the homeland of Japan, they were code named, **Pine**, since tree names were used for trainers. This design dates to 1929 and evolved over the years in numerous changes. So basic was the design that it was well suited for many types of airborne crew training that included flex-gunnery, navigation, radio communication, aerial photography and others. Room was sufficient for four students and an instructor. The pilot was seated in an open cockpit in front of the wing leading edge.

RANDY
Kawasaki Army Exp. High-altitude Fighter (Ki-102a)
Kawasaki Army Type 4 Assault Plane (Ki-102b)
Kawasaki Army Night Fighter (Ki-102c)

This airplane code named **Randy** made its first flight in March 1944 as an Army Assault Plane for the support of troops. In that capacity, **Randy** was first encountered by the Allies in the Okinawa campaign. As the war turned in greater disfavor for Japan, the need for an interceptor to counter heavy bombers became apparent. This airframe converted well to the air defense role in several armament configurations. Other structural changes were made in support of this new mission. Still other requirements were placed upon the design when the menace of B-29s had to be dealt with by night fighters. Modifications for this role included placement of obliquely mounted guns on the top and the bottom of the fuselage. The war ended before this version entered service.

RAY
Mitsubishi Navy Type 1 Single-seat Fighter
(See **Zeke**)

In the opening months of conflict, confusion in describing enemy aircraft by Allied crew members often resulted in two or more descriptions of one airplane. As a result, this sometimes led to assigning more than one code name to the same aircraft. When the Zero Fighter was sighted and reported in the CBI, it was assigned the code name **Ray**, not realizing that this was the same fighter to which the code name **Zeke** had been assigned in the SWPA. When the duplication was realized, the name **Ray** was cancelled in favor of **Zeke**. The name **Ray** was that of Captain Ray W. McDuffey of 5th Air Force Intelligence, close friend of Frank McCoy, who had early responsibility of assigning code names.

REX
Kawanishi Navy Fighter Seaplane Kyofu (N1K1)

This seaplane fighter proved to be the most effective of this type, world wide. This was intended as an air superiority fighter to support Japanese amphibious landing forces when air strips were not available. Before it entered unit service in the spring of 1943, captured Japanese documents revealed its planned existence and purpose of this airplane, therefore the nickname **Rex** was assigned before the aircraft was encountered. Early in its operational service when the war took on a defensive role for Japan, **Rex** was used more as an air defense fighter, defending some of the many Japanese island outposts. This was the basic design from which the **George** land-based interceptor fighter evolved.

RITA
Nakajima Navy Experimental 18-Shi Attack Bomber
Renzan (G8N1)

This bomber was recognized as a possible threat when first photographed on a flight line along side a **Liz** in the spring of 1945. That photograph provided relative size and configuration of this second type of Japanese four-engine land-based bomber. It was given the code name **Rita**, but was never encountered in combat although sightings of them on the ground were reported. The purpose for **Rita** was to support the long standing mission of land based bombers to support the Japanese fleet. As the development of **Rita** progressed, to make attacks against distant Allied bases became paramount. Only four prototypes were built for testing, and the war ended before its development problems were fully resolved. The shortage of construction material inhibited and later canceled production all together.

ROB
Kawasaki Army Experimental High-speed Fighter
(Ki-64)

The existence of what was code named **Rob** was learned through intelligence gathered data. This was to be a high speed fighter having two engines mounted in tandem and driving counter-rotating propellers. These engines utilized a steam vapor cooling system which incorporated the wing and flap surfaces for cooling areas, one side per engine. The threat of this fighter ended early when the rear engine of the prototype caught fire soon after its fifth in a series of test flights which began in December 1943. While repairs were underway, the airplane was declared too complex and the development program was terminated in favor of a more conventional design.

RUFE
Nakajima Navy Type 2 Fighter Seaplane (A6M2-N)

Early in the Pacific War, the Japanese Navy needed an interim seaplane fighter while the very advanced design of the Kawanishi **Rex** seaplane fighter was being developed. The Navy instructed Nakajima to configure the **Zeke** fighter, which they too were manufacturing along with Mitsubishi, to a single float seaplane fighter. This combination produced a very nimble and hard striking air superiority fighter. When the Japanese began their offensive in the Aleutian campaign, the Americans encountered this new fighter for the first time and gave it the code name of **Rufe**. When the **Rex** seaplane fighter came into unit strength, **Rufe** faded from the front lines and was used as a fighter seaplane trainer. It appeared in combat again in the closing months of the war while operating from its base on Lake Biwa, when it was utilized as an interceptor in the defense of the Osaka-Kyoto area of Japan.

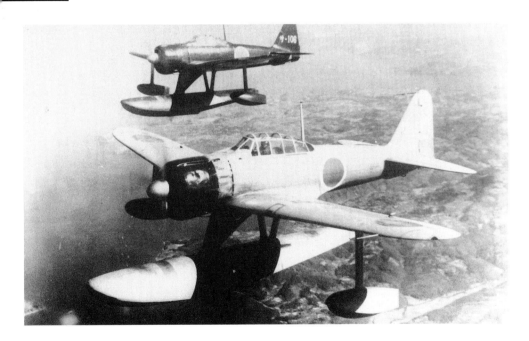

RUTH
Army Type I Medium Bomber (Fiat B.R.20)

The Japanese Army purchased 80 Fiat B.R.20 bombers from Italy in 1938 for their offensive in China. Known in Westerners terms as the "Mikado," these bombers were officially known as the Army Type I, "I" for Italy. Although they were modern and technically advanced at the time of their initial appearance in 1936, this twin-engine bomber quickly became outmoded. In their operations with the Japanese Army, they were found to be unreliable and were soon taken out of service. Their use by the Japanese had appeared in the news media of which Allied air intelligence took note and code named them **Ruth**. Since none had been encountered by Allied aircraft, these bombers were carried initially in the non-operational listing and finally deleted by mid-war.

SALLY
Mitsubishi Army Type 97 Heavy Bomber (Ki-21)
(See **JANE** and **GWEN**)

The versatility and widespread use of this bomber was cause for multiple code names being given to this one basic design. **Gwen**, **Jane** and **Sally** were assigned because of being reported on various fronts and having various armament configurations which made them appear as more than one type of bomber and transport. The name **Sally** prevailed, named after the wife of 38th BG commander, Fay R. Upthegrove, friend of Frank McCoy, the one initially in charge of the code naming system. Pre-war pictures of **Sally** were plentiful because of their extensive use in China and illustrated in Japanese magazines. **Sally** provided good service with the Army during the early months of the war, but became a notoriously easy prey for Allied fighters. Extended beyond its day, **Sally** was still liked by its crews for its ease in handling and maintenance.

SAM
Mitsubishi Navy Experimental 17-Shi Ko Type Carrier Fighter Reppu (A7M)

One of the many advanced designs and one that showed the greatest promise for late-war aircraft was the mention of this fighter in documents intercepted by Allied air intelligence. An illustration of the aircraft was not included, but with this information, the code name **Sam** was assigned. Initially intended as a carrier-based fighter, the concept was changed in February 1944 to that of a land-based interceptor which demanded a high rate of climb. But because of difficulty in developing the promised higher powered engine needed for this large fighter, the airplane was not developed beyond the prototype stage by the time the war ended. In its initial concept, this was to be a replacement for the **Zeke**.

SANDY
Mitsubishi Navy Type 96 Carrier Fighter (A5M)
(See CLAUDE)

Wide spread activity of this airplane gave cause for dual assigning of code names. **Sandy** was selected for this Type 96 Carrier Fighter when reported incorrectly from the CBI as the Type 97. It was therefore thought to differ from the Type 96 Carrier Fighter named **Claude** by air intelligence in SWPA. When discovered to be the same aircraft, the name **Sandy** was eliminated by June 1943. By then, even **Claude** had long been assigned to second-line duties, primarily that of fighter-trainer. This was a fighter that made its claim to fame in China.

SLIM
Watanabe Navy Type 96 Small Reconnaissance Seaplane (E9W1)

An airplane named early in the code naming system was **Slim**. This was a small biplane reconnaissance seaplane that was able to be carried aboard several classes of Japanese submarines beginning in 1936 as standard equipment. It was reported they could be assembled in 2-minutes 30-seconds, and dismantled in 1-minute 30-seconds. These were the last submarine-based Japanese biplanes of a long line of predecessors. Unknown to Allied air intelligence, these aircraft had been replaced starting in 1940 by the monoplane code named **Glen**. As a result, it is unlikely that **Slim** was ever encountered during the Pacific War.

SONIA
Mitsubishi Army Type 99 Assault Plane (Ki-51)

Described first as the Type 98 light bomber in recognition material, there was obvious confusion with the similar, but more robust, Mitsubishi Type 97 Light Bomber **Ann**, which in some cases was also reported as a Type 98. This was but one of the many examples of confusion over the number of single-engine, low-wing fixed landing gear that were in the Japanese stable of military aircraft at the beginning of the Pacific War. Once this airplane was specifically identified, it was given the code name **Sonia**. The airplane was a ground support light attack bomber capable of carrying an array of 12 bombs externally with two forward firing guns and a rear firing flexible machine-gun. This much used aircraft remained in production by Mitsubishi to March 1944 and Tachikawa to July 1945.

SPRUCE
Tachikawa Army Type 95-1 Intermediate Trainer (Ki-9)

Since trainers were assigned names of trees, this Ki-9 was labeled **Spruce**. These were in service before the Pacific War began, beginning in 1935, but not named until quite late in the war. It was not until Allied forces began to close on Japan that code names for non-combat types were considered appropriate. Some of this type could be anticipated to be seen in satellite countries of Japan and others to be used in kamikaze attacks in the invasion of Japan. **Spruce** could be considered a counterpart to the U.S. built Stearman PT-17/N2S Kadet series of primary trainers.

STELLA
Kokusai Army Type 3 Command Liaison Plane (Ki-76)

Ten months before the one Fieseler Fi 156 Storch was sent to Japan in 1941, design was started at the Army's request for a similar aircraft to do artillery spotting and liaison missions. The main difference in the two aircraft was that the Japanese version had a radial engine and higher power than the Argus powered German aircraft. Because of the power differential, the Japanese airplane exceeded the Storch in flight comparison with the exception of having a longer landing roll. The Allies did not know of this airplane's existence until June 1945 at which time it was code named **Stella**.

STEVE
Mitsubishi Army Experimental Fighter (Ki-73)

When intelligence sources were informed about the Ki-73 in 1944, indications were that it was about to enter service. This was to be a long-range escort fighter that would provide bomber protection for missions that were to attack U.S. bases. For this expected fighter, the code name **Steve** was assigned. Captured Japanese documents revealed it to have a 2,600 hp 24-cylinder horizontal-H liquid-cooled engine. This highly complex and very advanced engine had endless problems which caused this fighter concept to be abandoned. The sketch shown here is an interpretation of the design by Richard Bueschel.

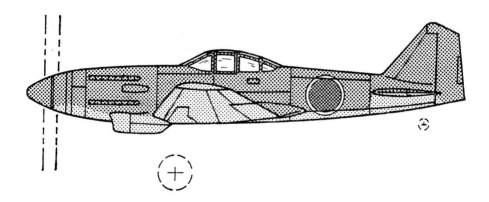

SUSIE
Aichi Navy Type 96 Carrier Bomber (D1A2)

One of the more stalwart Japanese Navy aircraft was this Type 96 Carrier Bomber. It was given the code name **Susie**. These basic-design biplane bombers first appeared in 1937 when attacking the gunboat *Panay* in China. The design of **Susie** was heavily influenced by the imported Heinkel He 66, a very effective German dive-bomber. These Aichi-built aircraft were carried on the initial Allied listing of Japanese aircraft as non-operational, since the opening phase of the Pacific War revealed to the Allies the state of modernization that had taken place with Japanese forces. They were, however, retained in Japanese Naval service as advanced trainers. Many of this type were fitted for kamikaze attacks had that final phase of the war materialized.

TABBY
Douglas Navy Type D Transport (L2D1) (DC-3)
Douglas Navy Type O Transport (L2D2/3)

Douglas DC-3s were not only imported into Japan in the late 1930s, but manufactured under license by Nakajima and Showa before and during the Pacific War. As a transport and therefore given an Allied code name beginning with "T" they were called **Tabby**. The origin of this name remains a mystery since this is a Japanese word for their single-towed mitten-like sock. Those who assigned these names are unaware of what prompted this name. There were slight recognition feature differences between the American DC-3/C-47 and the Japanese **Tabby**, mainly that the Japanese version often had an added window behind the cockpit and propeller spinners. This was one of four foreign design aircraft produced in Japan during the war years.

TESS
Nakajima-Douglas DC-2 Transport

Five DC-2s were imported into Japan as parts, and assembled by Nakajima. That company had obtained manufacturing rights for the DC-2 but did not exercise this right beyond the five assemblies because of the more advanced DC-3 that made them obsolete. They were given the code name **Tess**, since their existence in Japanese service was known and expected to be met in increasing numbers as military transports. Instead, only one DC-2 was used by the Army, the other four plus one imported aircraft were used as commercial airliners until all airline traffic came under the jurisdiction of the Army.

THALIA
Kawasaki Army Type 1 Freight Transport (Ki-56)

After exporting a number of Lockheed 14s to Japan in 1938, Lockheed sold manufacturing rights for this transport to Japan. Built in Japan by Kawanishi, that company later improved upon the design to be used as a military transport by lengthening the fuselage. Kawasaki was unaware that Lockheed had done the same lengthening of the fuselage (an additional 7-inches to that of the Japanese) in making the Lockheed 18 Lodestar. This new Japanese version went into production in 1940 with an enlarged cargo door, replacing the passenger door on the left side. As a Japanese Army Type 1 Freight Transport, it was given the code name **Thalia** when Allied air intelligence learned of the existence of this airplane. **Thalia** was often confused with the shorter version of the Lockheed 14 that was code named **Thelma**.

THELMA
Kawasaki-Lockheed Type LO Transport
(See **TOBY**)

Beginning in 1938, thirty Lockheed 14-38 "Super Electra" transports were exported to Japan for use on their domestic routes as well as those air routes linking Japan to China. At that time, the Lockheed 14 was touted as the worlds fastest airliner for its size, able to carry 14 passengers. It was soon adopted for military use by the Japanese Army, having both Kawasaki and Tachikawa produce the Lockheed 14 in its original configuration. This became the Army Type LO Transport. As the military transport, Allied air intelligence gave it the code name **Thelma**. This was the Japanese Army's standard transport, recognizing that many bombers were converted in large numbers to transport duties.

THERESA
Kokusai Army Type 1 Transport (Ki-59)

A seldom encountered aircraft was the Army Type 1 Transport. Failing in its design as a civil transport in the late 1930s, it became an Army transport beginning in 1941. When learning of the existence of this newly identified aircraft, Fran Williams of air intelligence unit in Australia named it **Theresa** after an Australian secretary within their organization. The characteristics of this airplane were disappointing and only a small number were produced, favoring the Tachikawa **Hickory** transport version instead. Since this was an unsuccessful high wing airliner, then became a military transport, this follows the same unflattering path as the failed Douglas DC-5 high wing civil airliner that resorted to becoming a military transport, the R3D for the U.S. Marines.

THORA
Nakajima Army Type 97 Transport (Ki-34)
Nakajima Navy Type 97 Transport (L1N)

This versatile transport was used by the Army, Navy, as well as a Japanese civil transport. Entering early service in 1937, it is surprising that it did not make the first listing of Allied code names for Japanese airplanes. It did appear as **Thora** in lists created as late as 1943. Except for an elongated nose, it was heavily influenced by the design of the Douglas DC-2 since Nakajima had manufacturing rights for that airplane. **Thora** went out of production in 1942, but their quantity was such that they remained in service until the end of the Pacific War and **Thoras** that were confiscated flew in China for a few years following the war.

TILLIE
Kusho Navy 12-Shi Special Flying-boat (H7Y)

In 1937, Japanese Navy requirements called for a super-secret reconnaissance flying boat capable of reaching the U.S. territory of Hawaii and return. The mission was so sensitive that the Navy created and built their own design within their Kusho facility. The airplane resembled the Dornier Do 26. Poor results with the one aircraft ended the project in 1939. Since the project was so highly classified because of its aggressive nature against the United States, all evidence that even supported the concept was supposedly destroyed. It is amazing that the Allies learned of this aircraft. Since they did, yet the uncertainty about its outcome was still present, it was given the code name **Tillie**.

TINA
Mitsubishi Navy 96 Transport (L3Y)

When Allied air intelligence realized that transport versions of the Navy Type 96 Attack Bomber were in civil transport service as well, they felt it appropriate to differentiate the transport from the bomber that was already code named **Nell**. They selected the nickname **Tina** for this transport version which appeared on their first listing of names. The telltale difference that identified **Tina,** other than the passenger windows, was mainly in the absence of gun emplacements and generally operating in natural metal finish.

TOBY
Kawasaki-Lockheed Type LO Transport
(See THELMA)

Having felt the need to distinguish civil airline Lockheed 14s over those used by the military, air intelligence assigned the name **Toby** to the civil-used Lockheed 14s. Three names now applied to the Lockheeds which caused undue confusion. The name **Toby** for the all-civil version was eventually dropped and **Thelma** applied to all standard Lockheed 14 type aircraft regardless of user. **Thalia** was retained for the Ki-56, stretched Lockheed 14.

TOJO
Nakajima Army Type 2 Single-seat Fighter Shoki (Ki-44)

This code name departs from the system developed that used western-world first names for naming Japanese aircraft. This Army fighter was first entered into the naming system in the CBI and pilots there called it **Tojo**. When the type was identified in the SWPA some time later in its operational service, it was given the code **John**. When the two names were learned to identify the same aircraft, the name **Tojo** was already well established by the CBI, and at their request official sanction was given for its continued use. The name **John** was short-lived as it was soon dropped for this aircraft. For **Tojo**, this was a vast departure from Army fighter requirements in that this airplane was designed as an interceptor fighter for area defense. First introduced in China in May 1942, this type remained in front-line Army service to the end of the Pacific War.

TONY
Kawasaki Army Type 3 Fighter Hien (Ki-61)

When the lines of this aircraft were first reported, they gave air intelligence strong indications that if these were not the expected Messerschmitt BF 109s flown by Japanese pilots, they must be an Italian design. Appropriately, the code name **Tony** was assigned. After closer encounters and later with ground inspection, it was realized that the airplane was an entirely new Japanese design. This was the first and only first-line fighter of Japanese forces that had a liquid-cooled in-line engine. When this was learned, it was easily recognizable. Engine problems curtailed deliveries until conversions were made with that of a radial engine. This changed **Tony's** lines considerably, but despite its redesignation to Ki-100, a new name was not assigned. **Tony** entered combat in April 1943 in New Guinea and remained in front-line service until the end of the war.

TOPSY
Mitsubishi Army Type 100 Transport (Ki-57)
Mitsubishi Navy Type 0 Transport (L4M1)

This airplane was known to exist before the war in 1939 and was frequently pictured as a civil transport. As the MC-20 airliner, it accommodated eleven passengers. The airplane was therefore given one of the early "T" names for transports, **Topsy**. Initial design was to satisfy Army requirements, having along side of it a civil version which diverted attention away from its sponsored military use. The Navy used **Topsy** transports as well after obtaining the Army's approval. **Topsy's** greatest notoriety came in February 1942 when this type discharged Japanese paratroopers for their invasion of airfields and oil refineries around Palembang in the Netherlands East Indies.

TRIXIE
Junkers Ju 52/3m Transport

Based upon reports that the Japanese were using Junkers Ju 52/3m transports, the code name **Trixie** was assigned. These reports were in error, and their origin may have stemmed from the visit to Japan made by one of these transports in May 1939. This was a goodwill flight made in an effort to cultivate greater trade relations with Japan. Allied air intelligence material that reported **Trixie** type aircraft as possibly being used by the Japanese, further described them as being glider-towing equipped.

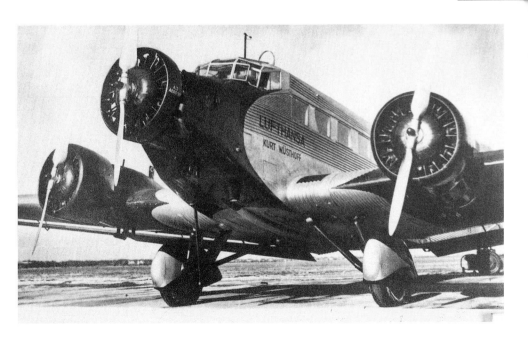

TRUDY
Focke-Wulf Fw 200K Kurier

A prominently reported German goodwill flight was made from Berlin to Tachikawa Air Base in November 1938 by a Focke Wulf Fw 200K Kurier. This visit is said to have generated Japanese Army interest in acquiring this type transport since it could be readily converted to a bomber. Nothing further developed, but because of this possibility of meeting Japanese-flown Fw 200s in the future, Allied air intelligence assigned the code name **Trudy** to this aircraft.

VAL
Aichi Navy Type 99 Carrier Bomber (D3A)

Used by the Japanese in the Pearl Harbor attack, **Val** was one of the first aircraft to be given a code name. To some, the name **Val** has a Tennessee twist, yet Val was the name of an Australian friend of McCoy's supervisor who made this request of name assignment. The airplane was described in two Models; **Val 1** was distinguished by having a rear stepped canopy, and for **Val 2,** the green house was faired into the fuselage. This aircraft looked obsolete from the beginning of its service in the Pacific War because of its fixed landing gear. Performance wise, it compared well with its U.S. Navy counterpart, the Douglas SBD Dauntless. When its replacement **Judy** came into service, **Val** was generally relegated to land-based units and to the smaller carriers not having adequate deck length for the faster landing **Judy.**

Code Named Japanese Aircraft Described

WILLOW
Kugisho Navy Type 93 Intermediate Trainer (K5Y)

This was the basic flight trainer for the Japanese Navy from 1934 through the end of the war. Named **Willow**, they warranted a code name since they would be expected to be seen as the Allies moved nearer Japanese shores. Many served in satellite countries of Japan as well. A number of these trainers were equipped with twin floats as seaplane trainers. When the Allies achieved victory and moved on to Japan, 8,000 aircraft, including these trainers had been converted to kamikaze attackers.

ZEKE
Mitsubishi Navy Type 0 Carrier Fighter (A6M)

Last but not least on the Allied code name lists was **Zeke**, the name assigned to the Zero Fighter. This Tennessee hillbilly name was a natural for this fighter that came into fame during the Pearl Harbor attack. While often referred to as **Zeke**, the name Zero Fighter persists as the most popular name of the two. It applied to all models of this famous fighter with exception of the short period that **Hap** and **Hamp** applied to the Model 32 Zero. At the onset of the war, the **Zeke** appeared to be invincible and carried that reputation in the opening months. When later model Allied aircraft appeared the newer Japanese types were few in numbers if available at all for various battles. Therefore the **Zeke**, although modified somewhat, had to be committed as the Navy's first-line fighter to the very end of the war.

Chapter III
Non-Code Named Japanese Aircraft

The Allied air intelligence community were aware of a number of obscure aircraft types and were included in their code naming program. Others slipped by, including late-war operational types that failed to be given code names. On the other extreme were the aircraft that had been obsolete for many years, yet were recognized with names.

It is appropriate, however, to note and illustrate the unnamed aircraft in order to have a fairly complete coverage of Japanese aircraft associated with this war-time period. Extremes will be noted, types that were very old, yet made their appearance, while others were the latest aircraft developments, obviously shrouded in deep secrecy. Some of these discoveries did not occur until Allied Forces moved on to the main islands of Japan after the war.

The following aircraft are those that did not receive a code name, yet are types that could have logically been named considering the pattern set by those that were responsible for the code naming system. This must not be construed as a definitive list, since many other aircraft could have been learned to exist by air intelligence, even if only in prototype or proposal stages as some were, and still given a code name.

Aichi Navy Type 2 Trainer Flying Boat (H9A1)

If known at the time, this aircraft would have had a "tree" name since it was designed as a flying boat trainer for Japanese crews that would man such aircraft as **Mavis** and **Emily**. They may have been reported as **Cherry**. These had a retractable beaching tricycle gear.

Aichi Navy Exp. 17-Shi Special Attack Seiran (M6A1)

Had the war continued for another 30-days without strong Allied advances, two large Japanese submarines carrying six of these bombers were prepared to bomb the Panama Canal. Designed for this purpose, they had other targets of which two submarines with 6 Seirans were converging upon Ulithe Atoll and the U.S. fleet when the war ended.

Aichi Navy Exp. 17-Shi Special Attack Nanzan (M6A1-K)

To provide training for crew members of Seiran, two of these Nanzan land based trainers were constructed. The top folding portion of the tail was removed to simulate lateral stability of the float equipped Seiran. The destructive capability of this weapon system was greater than historical records relate.

Fiat C.R.42 Single-seat Fighter

Alleged by someone that this Italian Fighter could be found in Japanese service, this photograph had been retouched with the Japanese insignia. Found in a recognition album of Japanese aircraft belonging to the American Air Attache to Germany just prior to World War II. Based upon this presence alone, it could have been eligible for a code name.

Kawasaki Ki-60 Army Experimental Fighter

Contrary to normal Army specifications for fighter maneuverability and extensive range, the Ki-60 was required to have speed and a high rate of climb for use as a heavy interceptor. Built around the DB 601A engine or Japanese version, the airplane development was not continued, favoring the Kawasaki Ki-61 **Tony**.

Ki-66 Kawasaki Army Experimental Dive Bomber

Having a strong resemblance between the Kawasaki's Ki-45KAI and Ki-48, this airplane was primarily a dive bomber. Six prototypes were built in 1942/43, but the Ki-48 **Lily** when modified for dive bomber duties performed nearly as well, and thus the Ki-66 was discontinued.

Kawasaki Army Ki-78 High-speed Research Plane

There were a number of one-of-a-kind aircraft or proposals of advanced designs that if known about, would have warranted a code name like those of the "dream aircraft." This Ki-78 failed to reach the high-speed research speeds it was designed to do, and therefore the project was abandoned in January 1944.

Kawasaki Army Type 5 Fighter (Ki-100)

Although frequently met in combat toward the end of the war, it is surprising that this Ki-100 was not given a code name. Although this is a radial-engine version of the Ki-61 **Tony**, it was never identified in recognition manuals as a derivative of the same aircraft having the same name.

Kayaba Army Observation Autogiro (Ka-1)

Although approximately 240 of these autogiros were built, little was known of their existence probably because they were Army Artillery Hq. equipment, and not part of Army Air Hq. Their mission was that of artillery spotting. This is a derivative of a Kellett KD-1A that had been imported into Japan for evaluation in 1939.

Kobe Army Type Te-Go Observation Plane

An airplane of which few were built, the type did exist as an Army observation aircraft. Its designation is not that of the Kitai system since the Army Artillery Hq. regarded this more as a "machine" for artillery spotting and not part of the normal aircraft inventories and certainly not part of the Army Air Headquarters.

Kugisho Navy Exp. 18-Shi Reconnaissance Keiun (R2Y1)

This aircraft held great promise in being a very fast reconnaissance aircraft. As the need shifted to that of a fast attack aircraft, its design was to be modified to a jet attack bomber. This prototype was powered by a six bladed propeller, but flew only one time before the war ended. A second prototype was nearly completed.

Kyushu Navy Operations Trainer Shiragiku (K11W1/K11W2)

One of few new designs to emerge during the Pacific War, this five place crew trainer was to be a replacement of **Pine**. Its non-retractable landing gear was usually un-spatted. Late in the war, many were modified to carry a single 551 lb bomb for kamikaze attacks for the expected invasion. Others were couriers after the war.

Kyushu Navy 18-Shi Interceptor Fighter Shiden (J7W1)

This concept of canard design as a fighter was being repeated with the Curtiss XP-55 Ascender in the United States at nearly the same time. The Shiden, however was planned to be produced while the XP-55 was not. Three short flights were made with the Shiden before the end of the war prevented further development.

Army Manshu Type 2 Advanced Trainer (Ki-79b)

Actually built in four trainer versions of the Ki-27 **Nate**, only this one had features that were noticeably different from **Nate** which made having a code name seem appropriate. Built in Manchuria, most served in training units in that distant location far from the combat areas and therefore not expected to be encountered.

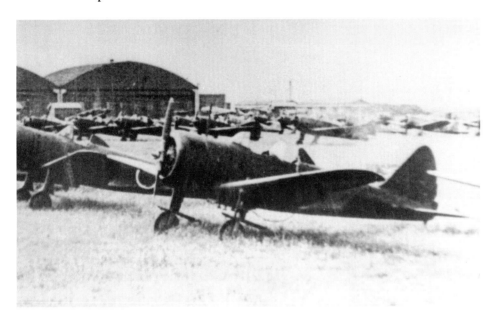

Mitsubishi Army Exp. Long Range Fighter (Ki-83)

Flight tests of this advanced long-range fighter design were frequently interrupted by Allied air attacks beginning in November 1944. Therefore, it is surprising this airplane was not spotted, reported and given a code name. Only four prototype were built then terminated since priority was given to home defence interceptors.

Mitsubishi Navy Type 2 Training Fighter (A5M4-K)

This trainer was a modified version of **Claude** having two seats to accommodate a student and instructor. A roll-over pylon was added between the two seats and wheel covers were deleted. Approximately 103 of these aircraft were placed in service between 1942 and 1944. They would have served as kamikaze aircraft against the Allied invasion.

Mitsubishi Navy Special Interceptor Fighter Shusui (J8M1)

Japan acquired manufacturing rights from Germany to build their Messerschmitt Me 163 rocket powered interceptor. Although visibly a Navy project, this was a joint Army-Navy development program intended to defend the Japanese home islands against air attacks. Flights were made for tests in glider versions before the war ended.

Nakajima Army Experimental High-altitude Fighter (Ki-87)

This was hoped to be a "super-fighter" because of its 2,400 hp engine which had a turbosupercharger. Many options in armament, power and self-sealing fuel tanks were being contemplated for the first ten prototypes. Problems with all these factors allowed for only one prototype to be built before the war ended.

Nakajima Army Special Attack Tsurugi (Ki-115)

Designed exclusively for kamikaze attacks to counter the expected Allied invasion, this airplane was planned to be manned by low experienced pilots. Difficulty of control however, required highly skilled pilots, yet production of these one-way aircraft continued until the end of the war. None were ever used in combat. Landing gear was jettisoned after takeoff.

Nakajima Navy Kikka

Japan entered the jet age with Kikka as their first jet aircraft. The design was based upon the Messerschmitt Me 262, but it became a scaled down version because of the loss of drawings that were otherwise intended for producing the German design. One successful and one aborted flight were made before the war came to a close.

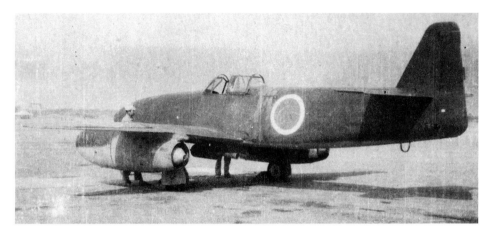

Nakajima Navy Type 95 Carrier Fighter (A4N1)

This was the last biplane carrier based fighter of the Japanese Navy, having been replaced by the **Claude**. Despite the generations of later types that evolved during the Pacific War, some of these fighters were retained as trainers, and were later modified for kamikaze attacks for the anticipated Allied invasion.

Nakajima Navy Type 97 Carrier Reconnaissance (C3N1)

Designed by Nakajima during the time **Kate** was being developed, flight evaluations for both types in China revealed that **Kate** could perform both tasks. Only two C3N1s were built. If seen while being flown in China, they could have been mistaken for the B5M1 **Mabel**.

Nakajima Navy Exp. 18-Shi Fighter Tenrai, (J5N1)

This twin engine fighter was designed as a replacement for the aging **Irving**. Two versions were being flight tested when the war came to an end; single-seat and two-seat configurations. Flight performance was disappointing, and therefore not put in production beyond the six prototypes.

Nihon Navy Exp. 13-Shi Amphibian Transport (L7P1)

Strongly resembling the Sikorsky S-43 twin engine amphibian, the L7P1 was smaller, and was intended to carry only eight passengers. First flown in 1942, the design was accepted by the Navy in 1943, but never recognized as an official type. Only the two prototypes were completed of Japan's only Japanese amphibian at that time.

Rikugun Ki-93 Experimental Ground Attack Aircraft

Only one of these aircraft were built when the war ended, but its existance may have been known to air intelligence as were so many other experimental types. Built by the First Army Air Arsenal at Tachikawa. Heavy armor plating protected the pilot and engines, and all fuel tanks were self-sealing with automatic fire extinguishing systems.

Savoia Marchetti SM.75 Transport

With the reported flight of this Italian transport to Japan in 1942, conclusions could have been reached by air intelligence that more were to follow, making a code name appropriate. This was the case with German aircraft going to Japan. This one aircraft returned to Italy as the only air contact made between Italy and Japan throughout the war.

Tachikawa Army Small and Light Ambulance Aircraft (KKY)

This airplane resembles the D.H. 83 Fox Moth, and was designed as an ambulance aircraft for the Army. Twenty-three were built beginning in 1933, and were widely used in air-evacuation duties during the Sino-Japanese conflict up to the early stage of the Pacific War, which made them appropriate for code name identification.

Tachikawa Army Long Range Research Aircraft (Ki-77)

As the Asahi A-26, this airplane was designed to make a goodwill non-stop flight from Tokyo to New York in 1940 for recognition of the 2600 year of Japan. Completion was delayed because of the approaching war, but after two were built, its range and endurance was proven in Manchuria. This design led to that of the **Patsy** bomber.

Yokosho Navy Type 3 Land-based Primary Trainer (K2Y2)

This primary trainer aircraft entered Navy pilot training service in 1932 and was built in large numbers for that purpose. Obsolete and superseded long before the Pacific War began, a number survived that war, particularly at satellite locations such as Manchuria. Many had previously been released for civil pilot training.

Yokosho Navy Type 90 Seaplane Trainer (K4Y1)

An airplane quite similar to the K2Y2 trainer was this airplane designed with twin-floats for seaplane training. To have assigned separate code names to these training aircraft that were so similar in appearance, particularly when seen in flight, would have expanded the code name list considerably.

Chapter IV:
From the Basics

This section reproduced here is the earliest known basic information relating to use of Japanese aircraft code names. It was published by the Directorate of Intelligence, Hq., Allied Air Forces, Southwest Pacific Area where these code names were created. Although the pages used are undated, the basic document with amendment instructions for new pages are dated July and September, 1942 respectively, the latter identifying the document as the third edition. Much of the early information contained in these source documents was fragmentary in itself, often using their own identifying system developed by air intelligence. This was necessary because of the complicated system the Japanese used in identifying their own aircraft, as well as incomplete information with which to prepare this intelligence material.

What is quite noticeable by its absence is a name assigned to this system of code names. According to Frank McCoy, the originator of the system and one who monitored it during its operational usage, he confirmed that the system did not have an official name, merely that of "Japanese aircraft nicknames" or "code names."

In order to provide background to the reader and researcher to this early material, and to have a better understanding of how this material was developed, the early listings from these consolidated documents, along with the instructions about them are reproduced here. They include entries made on change pages for updating these *Japanese Aircraft Manuals* as well as some of the superseded pages since they too contain early information that was later upgraded. By this time, in the first 3-months of using this new system, 78 of the eventual 122 nicknames had been assigned to Japanese aircraft.

Here then is a consolidated copy of these two early editions of the same document series which show only those portions that pertain to Japanese aircraft nomenclature, and their related Allied code names up to that time.[1]

*   *   *

Intelligence Information Memorandum
No. 12
Third Edition

JAPANESE AIR SERVICES
AND
JAPANESE AIRCRAFT

Not To Be Taken Into The Air

Directorate of Intelligence
Headquarters, Allied Air Forces
South-west Pacific Area
September 1942

*   *

INSTRUCTIONS

This publication is being constantly amended and additional pages will be continually forwarded. For this reason, it is vitally important that this Headquarters has an accurate up to date record of the proper address for every holder.

Pages are unnumbered intentionally (with the exception of a few numbered through printer's error which should be ignored). Thus replacement pages and additional pages can be inserted in any position, and those pages pertaining to particular aircraft can be shifted from operational to non-operational classification and vice versa.

LIST OF CONTENTS

Complete List of Japanese Aircraft
Japanese Air Services
Conversion Factors
Japanese Badges of Rank
Japanese Bombs and Armament
Japanese Tactics
Japanese Aircraft — operational in S.W.P.A.
Japanese Aircraft — non-operational in S.W.P.A.

INTRODUCTION

In this and all other publications of this Headquarters, a uniform name system is used. As will be seen in the List of Japanese Aircraft, the following order of identifying is used, i.e., Type, Classification and Code Name. Thus the most familiar Japanese fighter is denominated "Type 0 MK 1 SSF ZEKE." Emphasis must be placed on two facts; First that the code name is in no sense a complete replacement of the proper name: instead it is an excellent brief but positive reference to ONE particular type of Japanese aircraft, especially for use in signals and combat reports. This reference is true even though the particular type of aircraft may be made by more than one manufacturer and may be used by both the Army and the Navy Air Forces.

Secondly, while not alone the complete proper name in this Headquarter's system, it is definitely an essential part of the name. In the instance of ZEKE as in many others, it must be remembered that positive evidence has been repeatedly examined at this Headquarters to support the following facts.
 (a) That the Japanese never use the "OO" in naming these aircraft.
 (b) That it is known to be manufactured by both the Mitsubishi and Nakajima factories.
 (c) That Nagoya is a geographical location of one of the Mitsubishi factories, and the term "Nagoya Zero" is an erroneous method of naming the aircraft.
 (d) That the Japanese do not refer to their aircraft using the manufacturer's name, and certain evidence is at hand to the effect that such reference would only confuse them.

(e) That ZEKE is used by the Navy both from carriers and land bases, and that it also is used by the Army from land bases. [Author: The Army never used the Zero, learned soon after this erroneous report.]

The Type number of the Japanese aircraft indicates the year in which it was accepted by the Service. Type 97 for example, was derived from the Japanese year 2597 or our year 1937. Type 0, likewise, was derived from the year 2600 or our year 1940. Use of "00" or "01" is not considered accurate in view of factual information. In the case of type numbers applied to Army aircraft and experimental types, the above does not always hold true. Aircraft in this publication have been classified numerically according to type within each of the following classes of aircraft, i.e.–

Fighters (including float-planes)	Light Bombers
Observation and Reconnaissance (including float-planes)	Medium Bombers
	Heavy Bombers
Torpedo and Dive Bombers (including float-planes)	Flying Boats
	Transports

The distinction between Army and Navy aircraft which is sometimes made, is not used as a means of classification by this Headquarters. Instead that information is given on the individual aircraft Performance Data Sheet.

Methods of attack are based upon the analysis of the blind spot in each aircraft in relations to the sectors on the standard clock diagram shown herein. The most favorable direction of attack has been determined by the elimination of these sectors in which the enemy aircraft can bring effective fire to bear.

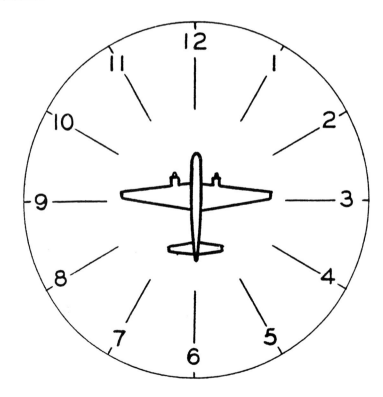

This data has been prepared by the Materiel Section of the Directorate of Intelligence, Headquarters, Allied Air Forces, South West Pacific Area. Any corrections or new details concerning its contents should be passed to that Section without delay.

THIS MEMORANDUM IS NOT TO BE TAKEN INTO THE AIR
DIRECTORATE OF INTELLIGENCE   September 1942

* * *

EXPLANATION

On the Performance and technical data sheet for each type aircraft [and code name listings], these abbreviations for type of aircraft are used:-[2]

SSF	–	Single Seater Fighter
SSF F/P	–	" " Float Plane
2E SSF	–	Two Engine Single Seater Fighter
2SF	–	Two Seat Fighter
O/P	–	Observation Plane
OF/P	–	Observation Float Plane
R/P	–	Reconnaissance Plane
RF/P	–	Reconnaissance Float Plane
T/B	–	Torpedo Bomber
D/B	–	Dive Bomber
DB F/P	–	Dive Bomber Float Plane
L/B	–	Light Bomber
M/B	–	Medium Bomber
H/B	–	Heavy Bomber
1E F/B	–	One Engine Flying Boat
2E "	–	Two " " "
3E "	–	Three " " "
4E "	–	Four " " "

JAPANESE AIRCRAFT - OPERATIONAL IN S.W.P.A.

FIGHTERS

Complete Name	Code Name
Type 97 SSF Nakajima	NATE
Type O MK 1 SSF Mitsubishi	ZEKE
Type O SSF F/P	RUFE
Type 1 SSF Nakajima	OSCAR
Type 0 MK 2 SSF (Square Wing Tip)	HAP
Type FW 190 SSF Focke-Wulf	FRED
Type ME 109 SSF Messerschmitt	MIKE

OBSERVATION AND RECONNAISSANCE

Type 95 RF/P Nakajima	DAVE
Type 96 RF/P (Small for submarine)	SLIM
Type O OF/P Sasebo	PETE
Type O RF/P (Small for submarine)	GLEN
Type O RF/P	JAKE

TORPEDO AND DIVE BOMBERS

Type 97 T/B MK I, II, III	KATE
Type 99 D/B Aichi	VAL
Type 99 D/B F/P	JUNE

From the Basics   167

```
                LIGHT BOMBERS
Type 100 L/B                        DINAH

                MEDIUM BOMBERS
Type 96 M/B Mitsubishi              NELL
Type 97 M/B Mitsubishi              SALLY
Type 99 M/B "Baltimore" Type ³      LILY
Type 1 M/B Mitsubishi               BETTY
Type   M/B (Short Nose)             DORIS
Type   M/B                          HELEN

                FLYING BOATS
Type 97 4E F/B Kawanishi            MAVIS
Type 2  4E F/B                      EMILY

                TRANSPORTS
Type 96 Transport                   TINA
Type 97 F/B Transport               TILLIE
Type D-2 (Douglas DC-2)             TESS
Type 1 Transport                    TOBY
Lockheed 14                         THELMA
MC 20 Mitsubishi                    TOPSY
Focke-Wulf Condor                   TRUDY
```

JAPANESE AIRCRAFT - NON-OPERATIONAL IN S.W.P.A.

```
                FIGHTERS
      Complete Name              Code Name
Type 96 SSF Mitsubishi          CLAUDE
Type 97 SSF Mitsubishi          ABDUL
Type 97 SSF Nakajima            CLINT
Type 98 SSF Kawasaki            PERRY
Type 97 SSF Mitsubishi Mitsu    SANDY
Type 97 2SF F/P Nakajima        ADAM
Type 98 2 SF Seversky           DICK
Type O 2E SSF Mitsubishi        HARRY
Type 1 SSF Mitsubishi           RAY
Type 1 SSF Kawasaki             JIM
Type   SSF Mitsubishi Mitsuto   BEN
Type AT27 SSF                   GUS
Type Suzukaze 20 SSF            OMAR
Type T.K. 4 2E SSF              FRANK
Type T.K.19 SSF                 JOE
Type Me 110 2E 2SF Messerschmitt DOC
Type He 112 SSF Heinkel         JERRY
Type 45 2E 2SF                  NICK

  OBSERVATION AND RECONNAISSANCE
Type 94 R F/P Kawanishi         ALF
Type 97 R F/P Aichi             BOB
Type 98 R F/P                   HANK

    TORPEDO AND DIVE BOMBERS
Type 96 D/B Mitsubishi          SUSIE
Type 96 T/B Nakajima            JEAN
```

```
Type 97 T/B Kawanishi Kawa          MABEL
Type 1 D/B Nakajima                 DOT
Ju 87B D/B Junkers Stuka            IRENE

            LIGHT BOMBERS
Type 97 L/B Kawasaki                MARY
Type 97 L/B Kamikaze                BABS
Type 97 L/B Mitsubishi Darai 108    NORMA
Type 98 L/B Mitsubishi              SONIA
Type 98 L/B Showa Sho 4             MILLIE
Type 98 L/B Mitsubishi              IDA
Type 1 L/B (ground attack) Nakajima JOYCE

            MEDIUM BOMBERS
Type 96 M/B Nakajima                EVE
Type 97 M/B Kawasaki Kawa           JULIA
Type 98 M/B Mitsubishi              LOUISE
Type 98 M/B Nakajima                BESS
Type    M/B unidentified            MAISIE
Type BR 20 M/B Fiat                 RUTH
Type Ju 88 M/B Junkers              JANICE
Type 98 B F/P Aichi                 IONE
Type O MB Mitsubishi                GWEN

            FLYING BOATS
Type 96 3E F/B Mitsubishi           BELLE
Type 98 1E F/B Aichi                LAURA
Type 99 2E F/B Kawanishi            CHERRY
Type 99 4E F/B                      JOAN

            TRANSPORTS
Ju 52 Junkers                       TRIXIE
```

Author's Notes:

[1] National Archives, National Records Center, Record Group 165, Entry 79, Box 1325.

[2] This early terminology was used in identifying other aspects of Japanese aircraft, i.e., recognition model programs, both plastic and wooden, as well as silhouettes of these aircraft used for training purpose.

[3] "Baltimore Type" described the Martin A-30 Baltimore bomber, supplied to the British.

[4] Showa refers to the time period of Showa in Japan and not the Showa Aircraft factory that had yet to be established.

Chapter V
Japanese Designations For Military Aircraft

A confusing aspect of descriptions for Japanese aircraft is embodied in the fact that the Army and the Navy each had two forms of aircraft nomenclature. In English usage, one form is called the **Long Title**, the other is the **Short Title**. *Seishiki Meisho* (the **Long Title**) means "Official (or accepted) Designation." The **Short Title** refers to two Japanese terms, *Ki Go,* meaning "symbols," and *Ryaku Go,* meaning "codes." A more descriptive term and common to both services is often translated to "Project Designations."

Very often, a researcher knows only one of these designations for a given aircraft and, therefore, needs a cross reference to the other system. For that reason, this reference book lists Official Designations and Project Designations in ways that allow the reader who knows only one designation to quickly trace the other designation and Allied code name.

OFFICIAL DESIGNATIONS
(Long Titles)

Both the Army and the Navy used a Type-number within their Official Designation for identifying their aircraft, yet each had subtle differences. The Type-number alone gave no clue to which service operated that aircraft, however. And in the early days of the Pacific War, this fact caused much trouble for Allied intelligence units and air organizations when the members referred to Japanese planes simply as Type 97's or as Type 96 bombers, and so forth. In this book, both Army and Navy Type-numbers are in a single list, in numerical order, with the service identified first.

Type-numbers derive from the last one or two digits of the Japanese calendar year in which the Japanese Army and Navy selected the design for service use. The Army and the Navy chose this year-type method for designating service aircraft beginning in 1927 and 1929, respectively. The numbering of the years by the Japanese calendar, called the national era system, comes from the Meiji Restoration of 1868, a system which retroactively numbered the years from the founding of the imperial dynasty, by tradition set at 660BC. The Japanese have used the system sporadically ever since then as a way of dating, much like that used with the Gregorian calendar system. As such, it had its greatest play in 1940 when the government celebrated what it proclaimed to be the 2,600th anniversary of the founding of the Japanese State.

In using this calendar system for dating aircraft by a Type-number, the two military organizations selected the last two digits, and later, only the last digit of the year in which the airplane was selected for use as a standard service aircraft. As an example, the Army Type 97 Fighter designation was derived from the Japanese year 2597, which also corresponds to our year 1937. The year before, 2596, the Navy adopted a Mitsubishi-designed carrier fighter which became known as the Type 96 Carrier Fighter. Any of the dates on the Japanese calendar can be converted to a Christian Era, or Gregorian calendar date by simply subtracting 660 from the Japanese date.

Beginning with aircraft numbered from the year 2,600, the Navy used only the last digit, thus the Zero Fighter got its name from Type 0, not 00, as was commonly thought by Allied nations to be the correct designation in the early days of the war. The **Betty** was a Type 1 Attack Bomber, having been accepted as an operational type by the Navy in 2,601 (1941), and the **Emily**, for one more example, became a Type 2 Flying Boat, accepted for service in 2,602 (1942).

At this juncture, the Army followed a different pattern for only a short while. Beginning at the year 2,600, some aircraft became Type 100, (logically following the Type 99 of the previous year 2599) such as the **Dinah**. But in the next year, the Army embraced the Navy idea and chose a single digit for the rest of the war years, i.e., Type 1 for the year 2601, Type 2 for 2602, and so forth.

There were cases where more than one Naval aircraft of a certain mission type was accepted in a given year, and therefore had to share the same Type-number. An example would be the Navy Type 90 Flying Boat built by Hiro and accepted in 1930. That same year Kawanishi also had their flying boat accepted by the Navy as an operational type. To distinguish between the two planes, the Navy added a suffix to the Type-number. It was a single digit, roughly equivalent to a "mark number," in western usage. Thus, the Hiro design became the Type 90 Mk.1 Flying-Boat (i.e. Type 90-1 Flying-Boat) and the Kawanishi design became the Type 90 Mk.2 Flying-Boat (i.e. Type 90-2 Flying-Boat). (Japanese usage: 90-*Shiki* 2-*Go*.) If there was a modification or even a second modification made to the Mk.2 aircraft, as example, an additional (Model) number was added. It appeared as Model 1 (1-*gata*), Model 2 (2-*gata*), etc., (i.e. Type 90-2-2 Flying-Boat).

Over a period from late 1942 to 1943, this form of identification changed when the Navy phased out the "mark number" system. Thereafter, the Navy used a two-digit model number. An example is the Type 99 Carrier Bomber Model 22 (stated as two-two, not twenty-two). The first 2 represents that a change had been made to the original production airframe. A further structural change would make it a model 32. The second 2 showed that the design firm had fitted a different engine from that of the original type.

When the design company made subtle changes that did not warrant a model-number change, the Navy added a Japanese symbol to the existing model number. The first six of these Japanese characters have been translated into Romanji as Ko, Otsu, Hei, Tei, Bo, and Mi. The Japanese use these as westerners use the letters of the alphabet, and the first six equate to a, b, c, d, e, and f, respectively. An example of this usage, in English translation, would be Navy Type 1 Attacker Model 24c (a late model of the **Betty**).

The designation system and sub-systems just discussed were used only after the particular aircraft was accepted as a service aircraft for the Navy. Since the development of such an aircraft was a Navy sponsored project, a separate system began in 1931 that was used during the time from issuing the Navy specifications for a given aircraft to the time it was accepted and given a Navy Type designation. That interim system was the Shi numbering system, short for *Shisaku Seizo*, literally meaning *trial manufacture*. The kanji character for Shi was prefixed by the Showa numbered calendar year and appeared as in this example: Experimental 10-Shi Carrier Attack Bomber, the 10 being Showa 10 or 1935, the year the specification was issued. When accepted, this same aircraft then became the Navy Type 97-1 Carrier Attack Bomber. This Nakajima-built aircraft (**Kate**) had to be Type 97-1 Carrier Attack Bomber, (having a -1 suffix) because Mitsubishi competed in the same specification category and their aircraft was accepted that year also. This became the Navy Type 97-2 Carrier Attack Bomber (**Mabel**).

Early in the Pacific War, popular names were bestowed upon some of the new Army airplane types placed into service in a gesture of showing pride and esprit de corps. Examples were Hayabusa (Peregrine Falcon for **Oscar**) and Shoki (Demon for **Tojo**). A department in charge of propaganda in the Army Ministry assigned these names to be able to mention them in press releases without giving true nomenclature. This name assignment action was totally outside the jurisdiction of Army Air Headquarters.

Japanese propagandists never linked the official or project designations to such names. And the respective military headquarters kept secret any consolidated listings of official or project designations from everyone who did not have a need to know the material. For this reason, air and ground crews seldom knew the names of their aircraft. Instead, they used military jargon and abbreviations such as "Ni Tan" for the **Tojo**. "Ni," the Japanese for "two," meant "Type 2" and "Tan," meaning "single," came from the descriptive term "single-seat fighter."

Factory workers were not much better informed. Plant personnel at Kawanishi, for instance, knew the N1K1-J Shiden (**George**) only as the "J," and the N1K2-J Shiden Kai as the "J Kai." But factory management staff and senior workers at Kawanishi knew and used the official designations for these two planes, Shiden Model 11 and Shiden Model 21 (or Shiden Kai). The "Kai" used here is for Kaizo, meaning "modification," and indicated a major change in the design, not a modification to an existing design. In the examples just given, the first design was the Shiden Model 11, followed by its highly modified successor, which was first known as the Shiden Kai during development, then as Shiden Model 21 when accepted for service use.

One thing that remained consistent throughout the war was inconsistency in Japanese aircraft terminology. Perhaps this unintentionally served for security of chronological aircraft data. It was not until 1945 that the Japanese Navy released a few aircraft designations to the public. The compromise was necessary because the air war had reached the home islands and the public had to have some knowledge of friendly and enemy aircraft.

By mid-1943 the Navy had abandoned its long-standing tradition of using type-numbers and mission descriptions in its official designations. Navy planners came up with a new system that made use of names and model numbers only, such as Shiden Model 11 and Shiden Model 21. Since only names and model numbers were marked on the aircraft, those captured by the Allies did not reveal to them when, or even if, the design had been selected for mass production and service use.

The Navy categorized the names of aircraft designed for certain missions. Special attack airplanes got names of blossoms, such as *Kikka* and *Ohka,* for Japan's jet fighter and the so-called Baka bomb, respectively. Attack bombers were named for mountains; night fighters, for light. Carrier fighter and fighter seaplanes got names derived from types of wind, such as *Kyofu* (Mighty Wind) for the **Rex** and *Reppu* (Hurricane) for the Mitsubishi A7M series called **Sam**. For lists of popular names, see Appendix A for Navy aircraft and Appendix B for Army aircraft.

The following list, titled *Japanese Army and Navy Aircraft by Type-number,* covers planes of the Pacific War along with older types that received Allied code names. The one-word name of the manufacturer and the project designation for each plane are included in a separate column, followed by the Allied code name.

Only the basic airplane type is represented in the column marked Official Designations. Modification suffixes do not appear. Some planes do, however, share the Type-number with other airplanes, and to distinguish them, a suffix number is attached to the Type-number.

A single asterisk (*) identified aircraft that did not actually exist, but that did receive Allied code names. Double asterisks (**) highlight duplications, where combat sightings and intelligence descriptions of various existing types got two or more code names before the Allies realized the data referred to a single design. These symbols follow the official designations.

Japanese Army and Navy Aircraft by Type Number

Official Designation	Mfg. and Project Desig.	Code Name
Navy Type 90 Operations Trainer	Mitsubishi K3M1	PINE
Navy Type 90-2 Flying-Boat	Kawanishi H3K1	BELLE
Army Type 93-2 Twin-engine Light Bomber	Mitsubishi Ki-2-II	LOUISE
Navy Type 93 Intermediate Trainer	Kugisho K5Y	WILLOW
Navy Type 94 Reconnaissance Seaplane	Kawanishi E7K	ALF
Army Type 95-1 Intermediate Trainer	Tachikawa Ki-9	SPRUCE
Army Type 95-3 Primary Trainer	Tachikawa Ki-17	CEDAR
Army Type 95 Fighter	Kawasaki Ki-10	PERRY
Navy Type 95 Reconnaissance Seaplane	Nakajima E8N1	DAVE
Navy Type 96 Carrier Fighter	Mitsubishi A5M	CLAUDE
Navy Type 96 Carrier Fighter **	Mitsubishi (See CLAUDE)	SANDY
Navy Type 96 Carrier Attack Bomber	Kugisho B4Y1	JEAN
Navy Type 96 Carrier Bomber	Aichi D1A2	SUSIE
Navy Type 96 Reconnaissance Seaplane	Aichi E10A1	HANK
Navy Type 96 Attack Bomber	Mitsubishi G3M	NELL
Navy Type 96 Transport	Kugisho L3Y	TINA
Navy Type 96 Reconnaissance Seaplane	Watanabe E9W	SLIM
Army Type 97 Command Reconnaissance Plane	Mitsubishi Ki-15	BABS
Army Type 97 Heavy Bomber	Mitsubishi Ki-21	SALLY
Army Type 97 Heavy Bomber **	Mitsubishi (See SALLY)	JANE
Army Type 97 Fighter	Nakajima Ki-27	NATE
Army Type 97 Fighter **	Nakajima (See NATE)	CLINT
Army Type 97 Fighter *	Mitsubishi	ABDUL
Army Type 97 Medium Bomber *	Kawasaki	JULIA
Army Type 97 Light Bomber	Mitsubishi Ki-30	ANN
Army Type 97 Transport	Nakajima Ki-34	THORA
Type 97 Light Bomber *	Mitsubishi	NORMA
Navy Type 97-1 and 97-3 Carrier Attack Bm.	Nakajima B5N1 & 2	KATE
Navy Type 97-2 Carrier Attack Bomber	Mitsubishi B5M1	MABEL
Navy Type 97 Flying Boat	Kawanishi H6K	MAVIS
Navy Type 97 Transport	Nakajima L1N1	THORA
Navy Type 97 Seaplane Fighter *	Nakajima	ADAM
Navy Type 97 Reconnaissance Seaplane *	Aichi	BOB
Army Type 98 Light Bomber	Kawasaki Ki-32	MARY
Army Type 98 Direct Co-operation Plane	Tachikawa Ki-36	IDA

Type 98 Medium Bomber *	Heinkel He 111	BESS
Type 98 Showa Light Bomber *	Vultee V-11GB	MILLIE
Navy Type 98 Reconnaissance Plane	Mitsubishi C5M	BABS
Navy Type 98 Reconnaissance Seaplane	Aichi E11A1	LAURA
Navy Type 98 Bomber Float Plane *	Aichi	IONE
Army Type 99 Twin-engine Light Bomber	Kawasaki Ki-48	LILY
Army Type 99 Assault Plane/Tactical Recon.	Mitsubishi Ki-51	SONIA
Army Type 99 Advanced Trainer	Tachikawa Ki-55	IDA
Navy Type 99 Carrier Bomber	Aichi D3A	VAL
Navy Type 99 S.E. Dive Bomber Seaplane **	Aichi (See JAKE)	JUNE
Navy Type 99 Flying-Boat	Kugisho H5Y	CHERRY
Navy Type 99 Four-engine Flying Boat *		JOAN
Army Type 100 Command Reconnaissance Plane	Mitsubishi Ki-46	DINAH
Army Type 100 Tactical Pilot Trainer	Mitsubishi Ki-46-IIKAI	DINAH
Army Type 100 Interceptor Fighter	Mitsubishi Ki-46-IIIKAI	DINAH
Army Type 100 Heavy Bomber Donryu	Nakajima Ki-49	HELEN
Army Type 100 Transport	Mitsubishi Ki-57	TOPSY
Army Type 0 Medium Bomber **	Mitsubishi (See SALLY)	GWEN
Army Type 0 Single-seat Twin-engine Ftr *	Mitsubishi	HARRY
Navy Type 0 Carrier Fighter	Mitsubishi A6M	ZEKE
Navy Type 0 Reconnaissance Seaplane	Aichi E13A1	JAKE
Navy Type 0 Small Reconnaissance Seaplane	Kugisho E14Y1	GLEN
Navy Type 0 Observation Seaplane	Mitsubishi F1M1	PETE
Navy Type 0 Transport	Douglas DC-3 L2D2/5	TABBY
Navy Type 0 Transport	Mitsubishi L4M1	TOPSY
Army Type 1 Fighter Hayabusa	Nakajima Ki-43	OSCAR
Army Type 1 Single-seat Fighter **	Kawasaki (See OSCAR)	JIM
Army Type 1 Advanced Trainer	Tachikawa Ki-54a	HICKORY
Army Type 1 Operations Trainer	Tachikawa Ki-54b	HICKORY
Army Type 1 Transport	Tachikawa Ki-54c	HICKORY
Army Type 1 Freight Transport	Kawasaki Ki-56	THALIA
Army Type 1 Transport	Kokusai Ki-59	THERESA
Army Type 1 Light Bomber *	Nakajima (See EVE)	JOYCE
Navy Type 1 Attack Bomber	Mitsubishi G4M1/G4M6	BETTY
Navy Type 1 Formation Escort Fighter	Mitsubishi G6M1	BETTY
Navy Type 1 Attack Bomber Trainer	Mitsubishi G6M1-K	BETTY
Navy Type 1 Transport	Mitsubishi G6M1-L2	BETTY
Navy Type 1 Target Plane	Kugisho MXY4	
Navy Type 1 Dive Bomber *	Nakajima (See JUDY)	DOT
Navy Type 1 Single-seat Fighter **	Mitsubishi (See ZEKE)	RAY
Army Type 2 Single-seat Fighter Shoki	Nakajima Ki-44	TOJO
Army Type 2 Two-seat Fighter Toryu	Kawasaki Ki-45KAI	NICK
Army Type 2 Advanced Trainer	Manshu Ki-79	
Navy Type 2 Training Fighter	Mitsubishi A5M4-K	
Navy Type 2 Fighter Seaplane	Nakajima A6M2-N	RUFE
Navy Type 2 Carrier Reconnaissance Plane	Kugisho D4Y1-C	JUDY
Navy Type 2 High-speed Recon.Seaplane	Shiun Kawanishi E15K1	NORM
Navy Type 2 Flying-Boat	Kawanishi H8K	EMILY
Navy Type 2 Training Flying-Boat	Aichi H9A1	
Navy Type 2 Land Based Reconnaissance	Plane Nakajima J1N1-C	IRVING
Navy Type 2 Gekko (Night Fighter)	Nakajima J1N1-S	IRVING
Navy Type 2 Primary Trainer Momiji	Kyushu K9W1	CYPRESS
Navy Type 2 Intermediate Trainer	Kyushu K10W1	OAK
Army Type 3 Fighter Hien	Kawasaki Ki-61	TONY
Army Type 3 Command Liaison Plane	Kokusai Ki-76	STELLA
Army Type 4 Heavy Bomber Hiryu	Mitsubishi Ki-67	PEGGY

Army Type 4 Special Attack Plane	Mitsubishi Ki-67-IKAI	PEGGY
Army Type 4 Fighter Hayate	Nakajima Ki-84	FRANK
Army Type 4 Primary Trainer	Kokusai Ki-86	CYPRESS
Army Type 4 Assault Plane (See note)	Kawasaki Ki-102b	RANDY
Army Type 4 Special Transport Glider	Kokusai Ku-8	GANDER
Army Type 4 Special Transport Glider **	Kokusai Ku-8 (GANDER)	GOOSE
Army Type 5 Fighter	Kawasaki Ki-100	
Navy Type D Transport	Douglas DC-3	TABBY
Navy Type He Interceptor Fighter	Heinkel A7He1	JERRY
Army Type LO Transport	Lockheed 14	THELMA
Army Type I Heavy Bomber	Fiat B.R.20	RUTH
Navy Type S Two-seat Fighter	Seversky A8V1	DICK

(Note: Type 4 Assault Plane was not officially designated. Some sources say "Type 5" for Ki-102b.)

PROJECT DESIGNATIONS
(Short Titles)

To identify experimental and development projects in an abbreviated form, the Army and the Navy went their separate ways once again. Each service devised project designations that were short, simple, and easy to use. Both services continued the use of these short titles even after a particular design received the official nod of approval and became an operational aircraft type, whereupon the design would get an Official Designation, too.

The Army set up its short title system in the 1930s. The system covered all aspects of aircraft equipment from airframes to bombs and airborne radios. The items in each of several categories received designations consisting of one Japanese symbol and a number chosen from a single chronological accounting list. The Army chose "Ki" for aircraft designs, Ki coming from Kitai, meaning "airframe." Engines got "Ha" from Hatsudoki, meaning "engine." "Ho" was the symbol for cannon, the "Te" was for machine guns. Gliders, being considered a special kind of aircraft, got designations with "Ku" as the abbreviation symbol for Guraida.

The Army retroactively applied the aircraft Ki numbers to a few designs that were still in the inventory. The Mitsubishi-designed Type 93 Heavy Bomber became the Ki-1, and the system progressed consecutively from there until some gaps appeared during the late Pacific War years. Some of the well known planes of World War II are the Ki-43, the Ki-44, the Ki-45, the Ki-61, the Ki-67, the Ki-84, and the Ki-100.

To the basic Ki number, the Army added Roman numerals to indicate a major modification and Roman letters to show sub-models. An abbreviation of the Japanese word "Kaizo," meaning modification, might also appear. For example, Ki-67-II identifies the second manor modification of the Ki-67 design. Adding a small "a" signifies a minor modification, Ki-67-IIa. The original Ki-45 was unsuccessful and was modified into the Ki-45KAI, with sub-models being the Ki-45KAIa, b, c, d, and e, indicating armament changes in these cases. In transliterated Army short titles, the word "Kai" is usually seen in all capital letters, so that a confusing array (such as Ki-45kaia) does not happen.

The Army kept its Ki-number system secret because it was sequential and it revealed the number of aircraft designs that had been developed. Even so, these Ki numbers were known to factory workers, pilots, crew members, and maintenance personnel because they were to be found on the name plates attached to various parts of an airframe, yet seemingly ignored in Japanese usage.

The Japanese Navy's short designation system was similar to that of the US Navy. They had admired the US Navy methods of operations as well as its airplanes from the early 1930s. As a result, they adopted the US Navy system of identifying its own aircraft. In its basic form, it consisted of four elements: (1) a mission-type symbol, (2) a one- or two-digit number showing a project's sequence within the mission category, (3) symbols to identify the designing firm (usually it was the manufacturer, as well), and (4) numbers and letters to indicate the particular modification.

The Japanese Navy used a Roman letter to identify the mission-type, followed by a one- or two-digit Arabic numeral which fixed the design's place in a sequence of designs within the mission category, then came one or two more Roman letters which identified the company that originated the design, followed by an Arabic numeral and sometimes a Roman letter to define the model.

To these four basic elements, the Navy added a dash and one or more symbols to show that an aircraft had been modified or adapted to perform a different mission from that originally envisioned for the type. When a basic airplane, for example the J1N1 **Irving**, no longer functioned as a Land-based Fighter as the "J" implied, but was now a Night Fighter having as a mission identifier "S", the short title became J1N1-S.

The letters denoting either the initial or the secondary mission appear with their definitions in the Navy Project Designations list that follows the list of Army designations. The letter or letters that indicated the designing firm – the second element in short titles – comes from this list:

A	Aichi Tokei Denki K.K., and Aichi Kokuki K.K.
	North American Aviation Inc.
B	Boeing Aircraft Company.
C	Consolidated Aircraft Corp.
D	Douglas Aircraft Company Inc.
G	Hitachi Kokuki K.K.
	Grumman Aircraft Engineering Corp.
H	Hiro Kaigun Kosho.
	Hawker Aircraft Ltd.
He	Heinkel (Ernst Heinkel Flugzeugwerke A.G.)
J	Nihon Kogato Hikoki K.K.
	Junkers Flugzeug und Motorenwerke A.G.
K	Kawanishi Kokuki K.K.
	Kenner Airplane & Motor Corp.
M	Mitsubishi Kokuki K.K.
	and Mitsubishi Jukogyo K.K.
N	Nakajima Hikoki K.K.
P	Nihon Hikoki K.K.
S	Sasebo (Dai-Nijuichi) Kaigun Kokusho.
Si	Showa Hikoki K.K.
V	Vought-Sikorsky Division of United Aircraft Corp.

W	Watanabe, K.K. Watanabe Tekkosho
	Kyushu Hikoki K.K.
Y	Kugisho (Yokosuka) (See note)
Z	Mizuno Guraida Seisakusho

Note: For the Pacific War period, Kugisho was the acronym used for Kaigun Koku-Gijutsu-Sho, meaning Naval Air Technical Arsenal, for aircraft designs emitting from this facility. Because of its geographical location at Yokosuka and the "Y" identifier, the term "Yokosuka" has become more widely used but is inaccurate. The earlier acronym; Kusho predates 1 April 1939, and before 1 April 1932, this was Yokosho, thus the origin of the "Y" designator.

Army Kitai Numbers

Ki-2	Mitsubishi Army Type 93 Twin-engined Light Bomber	LOUISE
Ki-9	Tachikawa Army Type 95-1 Intermediate Trainer	SPRUCE
Ki-10	Kawasaki Army Type 95 Fighter	PERRY
Ki-15	Mitsubishi Army Type 97 Command Reconnaissance Plane	BABS
Ki-17	Tachikawa Army Type 93-3 Primary Trainer	CEDAR
Ki-21	Mitsubishi Army Type 97 Heavy Bomber	SALLY
Ki-27	Nakajima Army Type 97 Fighter	NATE
Ki-30	Mitsubishi Army Type 97 Light Bomber	ANN
Ki-32	Kawasaki Army Type 98 Light Bomber	MARY
Ki-34	Nakajima Army Type 97 Transport	THORA
Ki-36	Tachikawa Army Type 98 Direct Co-operation Plane	IDA
Ki-43	Nakajima Army Type 1 Fighter Hayabusa	OSCAR
Ki-44	Nakajima Army Type 2 Single-seat Fighter Shoki	TOJO
Ki-45	Kawasaki Army Type 2 Twin-engine Fighter Toryu	NICK
Ki-46	Mitsubishi Army Type 100 Command Reconnaissance Plane	DINAH
Ki-46	Mitsubishi Army Type 100 Tactical Pilot Trainer (Ki-46-IIKAI)	DINAH
Ki-46	Mitsubishi Army Type 100 Intercepter Fighter (Ki-46-IIIKAI)	DINAH
Ki-48	Kawasaki Army Type 99 Twin-engine Light Bomber	LILY
Ki-49	Nakajima Army Type 100 Heavy bomber Donryu	HELEN
Ki-51	Mitsubishi Army Type 99 Assault Plane	SONIA
Ki-54a	Tachikawa Army Type 1 Advanced Trainer	HICKORY
Ki-54b	Tachikawa Army Type 1 Operations Trainer	HICKORY
Ki-54c	Tachikawa Army Type 1 Transport	HICKORY
Ki-55	Tachikawa Army Type 99 Advanced Trainer	IDA
Ki-56	Kawasaki Army Type 1 Freight Transport	THALIA
Ki-57	Mitsubishi Army Type 100 Transport	TOPSY
Ki-59	Kokusai Army Type 1 Transport	THERESA
Ki-61	Kawasaki Army Type 3 Fighter Hien	TONY
Ki-60	Kawasaki Army Experimental Fighter	
Ki-64	Kawasaki Army Experimental High-speed Fighter	ROB
Ki-66	Kawasaki Army Experimental Dive Bomber	
Ki-67	Mitsubishi Army Type 4 Heavy Bomber Hiryu	PEGGY
Ki-70	Tachikawa Army Exp. High-speed Command Recon. Plane	CLARA
Ki-71	Manshu Army Experimental Recon./Assault-Plane	EDNA
Ki-73	Mitsubishi Army Experimental Fighter	STEVE
Ki-74	Tachikawa Army Experimental Long-range Bomber	PATSY
Ki-76	Kokusai Army Type 3 Command Liaison Plane	STELLA
Ki-77	Tachikawa Army Experimental Long-range Research Plane	
Ki-79	Manshu Army Type 2 Advanced Trainer	
Ki-83	Mitsubishi Experimental Long Range Fighter	
Ki-84	Nakajima Army Type 4 Fighter Hayate	FRANK
Ki-86	Kokusai Army Type 4 Primary Trainer	CYPRESS
Ki-87	Nakajima Army Experimental High-altitude Fighter	
Ki-100	Kawasaki Army Type 5 Fighter	
Ki-102a	Kawasaki Army Experimental High-altitude Fighter	RANDY
Ki-102b	Kawasaki Army Type 4 Assault Plane	RANDY
Ki-102c	Kawasaki Army Night Fighter	RANDY

Ki-105	Kokusai Army Experimental Transport Ohtori	BUZZARD
Ki-106	Tachikawa Army Experimental Fighter	FRANK
Ki-109	Mitsubishi Experimental Interceptor Fighter	PEGGY
Ki-115	Nakajima Army Special Attacker Tsurugi	

(Ku = Guraida or glider)

| Ku-7 | Kokusai Army Experimental Transport Glider Manazuru | BUZZARD |
| Ku-8 | Kokusai Type 4 Special Transport Glider | GANDER |

(Ka = Kaitenyokuko or rotating wing aircraft. Not within Army Air Hqs. system since this aircraft was developed by Army Artillery Hqs.)

| Ka-1 | Kayaba Army Model 1 Observation Autogiro | |

Navy Project Designations

A - Carrier Fighter

A5M1/A5M4	Mitsubishi Navy Type 96 Carrier Fighter	CLAUDE
A6M1/A6M8	Mitsubishi Navy Type 0 Carrier Fighter	ZEKE
A6M2-N	Nakajima Navy Type 2 Fighter Seaplane	RUFE
A6M3	Mitsubishi Navy Type 0 Carrier Fighter Model 32	HAMP
A7M1/A7M3	Mitsubishi Navy Exp Carrier Fighter Reppu	SAM
A7He1	Heinkel Navy Type He Intercepter Fighter	JERRY
A8V1	Seversky Navy Type S Two-Seat Fighter	DICK

B - Carrier Attack Bomber

B4Y1	Kugisho Navy Type 96 Carrier Attack Bomber	JEAN
B5M1	Mitsubishi Navy Type 97-2 Carrier Attack Bomber	MABEL
B5N1/B5N2	Nakajima Navy Type 97-1 and -3 Carrier Attack Bomber	KATE
B6N1/B6N3	Nakajima Navy Carrier Attack Bomber Tenzan	JILL
B7A1/B7A3	Aichi Navy Carrier Attack Bomber Ryusei	GRACE

C - Reconnaissance Plane

| C5M1/C5M2 | Mitsubishi Navy Type 98 Reconnaissance Plane | BABS |
| C6N1/C6N3 | Nakajima Navy Carrier Reconnaissance Plane Saiun | MYRT |

D - Carrier Bomber

D2A1	Aichi Navy Type 96 Carrier Bomber	SUSIE
D3A1/D3A2	Aichi Navy Type 99 Carrier bomber	VAL
D4Y1-C	Kugisho Navy Type 2 Carrier Reconnaissance Plane	JUDY
D4Y1/D4Y5	Kugisho Navy Carrier Bomber Suisei	JUDY

E - Reconnaissance Seaplane

E2N1/E2N2	Nakajima Navy Type 15 Reconnaissance Seaplane	BOB
E7K1/E7K2	Kawanishi Navy Type 94 Reconnaissance Seaplane	ALF
E8N1	Nakajima Navy Type 95 Reconnaissance Seaplane	DAVE
E9W1	Watanabe Navy Type 96 Small Reconnaissance Seaplane	SLIM
E10A1	Aichi Navy Type 96 Reconnaissance Seaplane	HANK
E11A1	Aichi Navy Type 98 Reconnaissance Seaplane	LAURA
E13A1	Aichi Navy Type 0 Reconnaissance Seaplane	JAKE
E14Y1	Kugisho Navy Type 0 Small Reconnaissance Seaplane	GLEN
E15K1	Kawanishi Navy Type 2 High-speed Recon Seaplane Shiun	NORM
E16A1/A2	Aichi Navy Reconnaissance Seaplane Zuiun	PAUL

F - Observation Seaplane

| F1M1/F1M2 | Mitsubishi Navy Type 0 Observation Seaplane | PETE |

G - Attack Bomber

| G3M1/G3M3 | Mitsubishi Navy Type 96 Attack Bomber | NELL |
| G4M1/G4M3 | Mitsubishi Navy Type 1 Attack Bomber | BETTY |

G5N1/G5N2	Nakajima Navy Exp. 13-Shi Attack Bomber Shinzan	LIZ
G6M1	Mitsubishi Navy Type 1 Formation Escort Fighter	BETTY
G6M1-K	Mitsubishi Navy Type 1 Attack Bomber Trainer	BETTY
G6M1-L2	Mitsubishi Navy Type 1 Transport	BETTY
G8N1	Nakajima Navy Exp. 18-Shi Attack Bomber Renzan	RITA

H - Flying-Boat

H3K1/K3K2	Kawanishi Navy Type 90-2 Flying-Boat	BELLE
H5Y1/H5Y2	Kugisho Navy Type 99 Flying-Boat	CHERRY
H6K1/H6K5	Kawanishi Navy Type 97 Flying-Boat	MAVIS
H6K2-L	Kawanishi Navy Type 97 Transport Flying-Boat	MAVIS
H7Y1	Kusho Navy 12-Shi Special Flying-Boat	TILLIE
H8K1/H8K4	Kawanishi Navy Type 2 Flying-Boat	EMILY
H8K2-L	Kawanishi Navy Transport Flying-Boat Seiku	EMILY
H9A1	Aichi Navy Type 2 Training Flying-Boat	

J - Land-based Fighter

J1N1-R	Nakajima Navy Type 2 Land Based Reconnaissance Plane	IRVING
J1N1-S	Nakajima Navy Type 2 Gekko (Night Fighter)	IRVING
J2M1/J2M7	Mitsubishi Navy Interceptor Fighter Raiden	JACK
J4M1	Mitsubishi Navy Exp. 17-Shi Interceptor	LUKE
J5N1	Nakajima Navy Exp Interceptor Fighter Tenrai	
J7W1/J7W2	Kyushu Navy Exp 18-Shi Interceptor Fighter Shinden	
J8M1	Mitsubishi Navy Exp 19-Shi Interceptor Fighter Shusui	

K - Trainer

K3M1/K3M3	Mitsubishi Navy Type 90 Crew Trainer	PINE
K5Y1/K5Y5	Kugisho Navy Type 93 Intermediate Trainer	WILLOW
K9W1	Kyushu Navy Type 2 Primary Trainer Momiji	CYPRESS
K10W1	Kyushu Navy Type 2 Intermediate Trainer	OAK
K11W1	Kyushu Navy Operations Trainer Shigariku	

L - Transport

L1N1	Nakajima Navy Type 97 Transport	THORA
L2D1	Douglas Navy Type D Transport (DC-3)	TABBY
L2D2/L2D5	Douglas Navy Type 0 Transport	TABBY
L3Y1/L3Y2	Kugisho Navy Type 96 Transport	TINA
L4M1	Mitsubishi Navy Type 0 Transport	TOPSY

M - Special Mission

M6A1	Aichi Navy Special Attack Bomber Seiran	
M6A1-K	Aichi Special Attack Training Bomber Nanzan	

N - Fighter Seaplane

N1K1/N1K2	Kawanishi Navy Fighter Seaplane Kyofu	REX
N1K1-J	Kawanishi Navy Interceptor Fighter Shiden	GEORGE
N1K2-J	Kawanishi Navy Interceptor Fighter Shiden KAI	GEORGE

P - Bomber

P1Y1/P1Y6	Kugisho Navy bomber Ginga	FRANCES
P1Y1-S	Kugisho Navy Night Fighter Byakko	FRANCES
P1Y2-S	Kugisho Navy Night Fighter Kyokko	FRANCES

Q - Patrol Plane

Q1W1/Q1W2	Kyushu Navy Patrol Plane Tokai	LORNA

R - Land-based Reconnaissance

R1Y1	Kugisho Navy Exp. 17-Shi Reconnaissance Plane Seiun	

S - Night Fighter
(Aircraft type not sufficiently developed)

APPENDIX A:
Popular Names of Japanese Naval Aircraft

Carrier and/or Seaplane Fighter — Wind

Kyofu (Strong Wind)	N1K1	REX
Reppu (Violent Wind)	A7M1/2	SAM
Sukukaze (Cool Breeze)		OMAR

Land-based Interceptor Fighter — Thunder and Lightning

Jinpu (Squall)	J6K1	
Raiden (Thunderbolt)	J2M1/7	JACK
Senden (Flashing Lightning)	J4M1	
Shiden (Violet Lightning)	N1K1-J	GEORGE
Shinden (Magnificent Lightning)	J7W1	
Tenrai (Heavenly Thunder)	J5N1	

Night Fighter — Light

Byakko (White Light	P1Y1-S	FRANCES
Denko (Bolt of Light)	S1A1	
Gekko (Moonlight)	J1N1-S	IRVING
Kyokko (Aurora)	P1Y1-S	FRANCES

Bomber — Stars

Ginga (Milky Way)	P1Y1/6	FRANCES
Myojo (Venus)	D3Y1	
Ryusei (Shooting Star)	B7A1/3	GRACE
Suisei (Comet)	D4Y1/5	JUDY

Attack Bombers — Mountains

Fugaku (Mount Fuji)	G10N1	
Nanzan (Southern Mountain)	M6A1-K	
Renzan (Mountain Range)	G8N1	RITA
Seiran (Mountain Haze)	M6A1	
Shinzan (Mountain Recess	G5N1/2	LIZ
Taizan (Great Mountain	G7M1	
Tenzan (Heavenly Mountain)	B6N1/3	JILL
Tozan (Eastern Mountain)	Exp. Attack Plane	

Special Attack (Kamekaze) Planes — Blossoms

Baika (Plun Blossom)	Exp. Special Attacker	
Kikka (Orange Blossom)	Exp. Special Attacker	
Ohka (Cherry Blossom)		BAKA BOMB
Toka (Wistaria)	Exp. Special Attacker	
Baika (Plum Blossom)	Exp. Special Attacker	

Reconnaissance and Seaplanes — Clouds

Keiun (Beautiful Cloud)	R2Y1/2	
Saiun (Painted Cloud)	C6N1/3	MYRT
Shiun (Violet Cloud)	E15K1	NORM
Zuiun (Auspicious Cloud)	E16A1	PAUL

Transports — Sky
        Seiku (Clear Sky)   H8K2-L   EMILY
        Soku (Blue Sky)   H11K1-L

Trainers — Grasses or Trees
        Akigusa (Autumn Grass)   MXY8
        Momiji (Maple)   K9W1
        Shiragiku (White Chrysanthemum) K11W1
        Wakakusa (Young Grass)   Navy Primary Glider
        Wakazakura (Young Cherry)   MXY7-K2   BAKA

Land-based Patrol Aircraft — Sea
        Nankai (South Sea)   Q3W1
        Taiyo (Ocean)   Q2M1

APPENDIX B:
Popular Names of Japanese Army Aircraft

Donryu (Storm Dragon)	Ki-49	HELEN
Hayabusa (Peregrine Falcon)	Ki-43	OSCAR
Hayate (Gale)	Ki-84	FRANK
Hien (Swallow)	Ki-61	TONY
Hiryu (Flying Dragon	Ki-67	PEGGY
Karigane (Wild Goose)	Ki-15/C5M2	BABS
Shoki (Demon)	Ki-44	TOJO
Toryu (Dragon Killer)	Ki-45	NICK
Tsurugi (Sabre)	Ki-115	
Yasukuni (Shrine name)	Ki-67	PEGGY

NOTES

NOTES

NOTES

NOTES

NOTES

NOTES

NOTES

Also from the Publisher

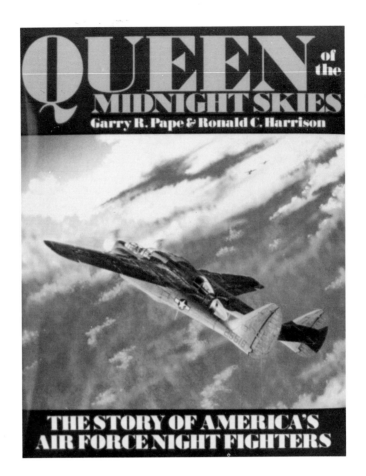

QUEEN OF THE MIDNIGHT SKIES
The Story of America's Air Force Night Fighters

Garry R. Pape & Ronald C. Harrison

Size: 8 1/2" x 11"   368 pages   hard cover   over 650 photos $45.00

INNOVATIONS IN AIRCRAFT CONSTRUCTION

Thirty-Seven Influential Designs

Wright Flyer
Junkers J1
Fokker Dr.I
Junkers Ju 52
Polikarpov I-16
Messerschmitt Bf 109
Boeing B-17
Douglas DC-3/C-47
Messerschmitt Bf 110
Junkers Ju 88
Macchi MC.200-207
Messerschmitt Me 209
Nakajima Ki-43 Hayabusa
Lockheed P-38 Lightning
Heinkel He 178
Hawker Tornado/Typhoon
Ilyushin Il-2 Sturmovik
Arado Ar 240
Chance Vought F4U Corsair
North American P-51 Mustang
DeHavilland Mosquito
Messerschmitt Me 262
Hawker Tempest
Arado Ar 234
Dornier Do 335
Republic F-84F Thunderstreak
Hawker Hunter
North American F-100 Super Sabre
Lockheed F-104 Starfighter
Saab J35 Draken
Vought F-8 Crusader
Mikoyan/Gurevich MiG-21
Dassault-Breguet Mirage III/5
Northrop T-38 Talon
Hawker Siddeley Harrier
Dornier Do 31
Aérospatiale/BAC Concorde

Hans Redemann

INNOVATIONS IN AIRCRAFT CONSTRUCTION

37 Influential Designs

Hans Redemann

Size: 8 1/2" x 11"   248 pages   hard cover   over 300 photos $29.95

JAPANESE   AIRCRAFT

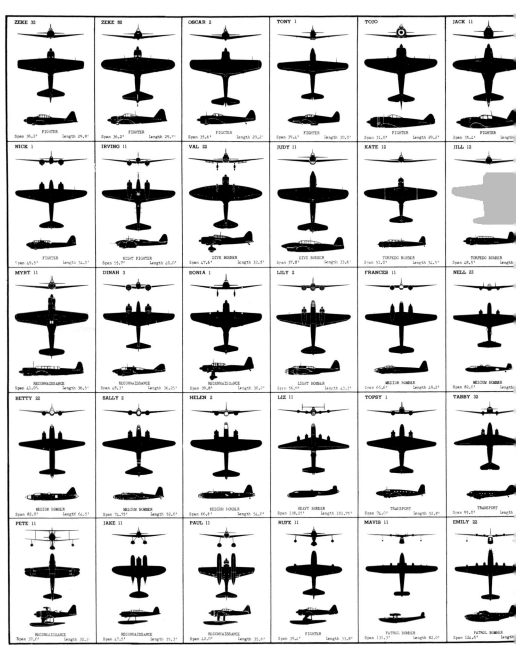

ZEKE 32	ZEKE 52	OSCAR 2	TONY 1	TOJO	JACK 11
FIGHTER	FIGHTER	FIGHTER	FIGHTER	FIGHTER	FIGHTER
Span 36.2' Length 29.8'	Span 36.2' Length 29.8'	Span 35.6' Length 29.2'	Span 39.4' Length 30.0'	Span 31.0' Length 29.2'	Span 35.4' Length

NICK 1	IRVING 11	VAL 22	JUDY 11	KATE 12	JILL 12
FIGHTER	NIGHT FIGHTER	DIVE BOMBER	DIVE BOMBER	TORPEDO BOMBER	TORPEDO BOMBER
Span 49.5' Length 34.5'	Span 55.7' Length 40.0'	Span 47.6' Length 32.9'	Span 37.8' Length 33.6'	Span 51.0' Length 34.5'	Span 48.5' Length

MYRT 11	DINAH 3	SONIA 1	LILY 2	FRANCES 11	NELL 23
RECONNAISSANCE	RECONNAISSANCE	RECONNAISSANCE	LIGHT BOMBER	MEDIUM BOMBER	MEDIUM BOMBER
Span 42.0' Length 36.5'	Span 48.3' Length 36.25'	Span 39.8' Length 30.2'	Span 56.9' Length 43.3'	Span 65.6' Length 49.2'	Span 82.0' Length

BETTY 22	SALLY 2	HELEN 2	LIZ 11	TOPSY 1	TABBY 32
MEDIUM BOMBER	MEDIUM BOMBER	MEDIUM BOMBER	HEAVY BOMBER	TRANSPORT	TRANSPORT
Span 82.0' Length 64.5'	Span 74.75' Length 52.0'	Span 66.6' Length 54.0'	Span 138.25' Length 101.75'	Span 74.0' Length 52.8'	Span 95.0' Length

PETE 11	JAKE 11	PAUL 11	RUFE 11	MAVIS 11	EMILY 22
RECONNAISSANCE	RECONNAISSANCE	RECONNAISSANCE	FIGHTER	PATROL BOMBER	PATROL BOMBER
Span 37.0' Length 32.3'	Span 47.5' Length 35.3'	Span 42.0' Length 35.6'	Span 39.4' Length 33.8'	Span 131.3' Length 82.0'	Span 124.6' Length